S0-ACW-088

TAKE THE RICH OFF WELFARE

MARK ZEPEZAUER
& ARTHUR NAIMAN

Odonian Press

distributed through

Common Courage Press / LPC Group

Additional copies of this and other Odonian Press Real Story books are available at most good bookstores, or directly from Common Courage Press. For a list of other titles, and details on ordering, see the inside back cover. To order by credit card, or for information on quantity discounts, please:

- call 207 525 0900 or 800 497 3207
- fax 207 525 3068
- email *odonian@realstory.com*
- visit the Odonian website at *www.realstory.com*
- write Common Courage at Box 702, Monroe ME 04951

Distribution to the book trade is through LPC Group, 1436 W. Randolph St, Chicago IL 60607. To order, call 800 243 0138. Real Story books are also available through wholesalers.

Copyediting and proofreading: **Susan McCallister**

Design, layout and glossary: **Arthur Naiman**

Recommended reading and sources: **Mark Zepezauer**

Legal vetting: **Alexander Greenfeld**   Index: **Paul Augspurger**

Cover illustration: **Debbie Jensen-Molnar**

Fonts: Ed Benguiat's **Bookman** (text), William Morris' **Liberty** (heads, etc.), Hermann Zapf's **Optima** (lists, etc.)

Series editor: **Arthur Naiman**

Copyright © 1996 by Odonian Press. All rights reserved, including the right to reproduce or copy this book, or any portions of it, in any manner whatever (except for excerpts in reviews).

Printed in the USA   Third printing—November, 1998

Library of Congress Catalog Card Number: 96-34351

**An Odonian Press Real Story book
published through Common Courage Press / LPC Group**

Odonian Press gets its name from Ursula Le Guin's wonderful novel *The Dispossessed* (though we have no connection with Ms. Le Guin or any of her publishers). The last story in her collection *The Wind's Twelve Quarters* also features the Odonians (and Odo herself).

Odonian Press donates at least 10% of its aftertax income to organizations working for social justice.

ACKNOWLEDGMENTS

Mark wants to thank Nan, Mom and Dad, Marvin & Carroll, the Enchilada Faceplants, and David Blaisdell; a small army of think tankers including Janice Shields, Bob McIntyre, Chuck Collins, Gawain Kripke, Russell Mokhiber, John Pike, Bill Wagner and others too numerous to mention; the helpful and patient reference staff of the Tucson Public Library; plus Matt Somers, Chaz Bufe, Chuck and Laurie; echinacea and goldenseal, Netscape, Alta Vista, George Seldes and the Pixies.

Arthur wants to thank Meg, Janee, Marty, Ira, Bonnie and Linda; SQ, Alex, Jim, JK, Richard, RCD, Charlie, Kristen, Gar, Randy and Teri; Lara and Rae; Mega, Bill and Jim; Ann, Mark, Darleen and Laura; Nettie, Chuck, Julie and Amanda; Barb, Rich, Kenny, Shari and Scott; and especially Rita, the Queen of the Family.

Much as we'd like to take credit for the title of this book, it was a campaign slogan used by Senator Fred Harris of Oklahoma when he ran for the Democratic presidential nomination in 1976. (Too bad he didn't win.)

ABOUT THE AUTHORS

Mark Zepezauer is the author of *The CIA's Greatest Hits* (also in the Real Story series) and *The Nixon Saga,* and is also the editor and publisher of *The Tucson Comic News.* He can be reached at *comicnews@earthlink.net* or at *http://tucson.com/ComicNews.*

Arthur Naiman's fourteen books have sold well over a million copies. He's also edited more than a dozen political books for Odonian Press.

CONTENTS

INTRODUCTION

Wealthfare—the money we hand out to corporations and wealthy individuals—costs us at least $448 billion a year. Let's put that number into perspective:

- The federal deficit—the amount the government's expenditures exceed its revenues—is now running about $117 billion a year (all figures on this page are for fiscal 1996). So we could wipe out the entire deficit simply by cutting wealthfare by about 26%.

- Welfare for the rich costs us about $3\frac{1}{2}$ times as much as the $130 billion we spend each year on welfare for the poor—an amount the 1996 welfare "reform" bill will reduce significantly. (For details on the programs that make up welfare for the poor, see the appendix that starts on page 157.)

- The federal budget's discretionary spending—in other words, not counting entitlement trust funds like Social Security and Medicare—is $1.23 trillion. So three years of wealthfare costs us more than it does to run the government for a year.

- The federal debt, which has been accumulating since 1789, is now about $5.1 trillion. So just $11\frac{1}{3}$ years of welfare for the rich equals more than 200 years of deficit spending by the whole federal government.

For a summary of what goes into that $448-billion wealthfare figure, turn back one page to the table of contents, where we list the estimated annual cost of the various subsidies, handouts, tax breaks, loopholes, rip-offs and scams this book describes.

6

We've calculated these amounts as precisely as possible, but since they change every year—and since data is often hard to obtain—they're inevitably estimates. But you could cut them all by 75% and welfare for the rich would still cost almost as much each year as the federal deficit.

We're not saying that $448-billion figure is an overestimate—if anything, it's an *under*estimate. Time and space limitations forced us to leave out many major categories of wealthfare.

Most of these could be books in themselves: state and local wealthfare (as opposed to federal), the easy treatment given white-collar criminals, Medicare waste and fraud, automobile subsidies, the effects of Federal Reserve policies, the NAFTA and GATT treaties, foreign aid, deregulation of various industries, fraudulent charitable deductions, and on and on.

We discuss some of them in the chapter called *What we've left out,* which begins on page 115. (Only the Pentagon chapter is longer, which gives you an idea of how much wealthfare isn't included in our estimate.)

Even within categories we do cite figures for, there are often additional wealthfare expenses we haven't been able to nail down. So, in our view, $448 billion greatly understates the amount of money American taxpayers spend each year on welfare for the rich.

Stealing from the poor
Before we go on, we'd like to make something clear. We're not saying there's anything wrong with being rich, in and of itself. Many wealthy

7

people earned their money by producing a product or service the public liked and wanted to buy, or by helping a company do that. The Grateful Dead are a good example—their concerts became so popular that they had to run lotteries to decide who got to buy tickets.

Now, speaking personally, we don't think people should inherit fortunes while others spend their whole lives scrambling to get by. We also think that, as long as anybody in the world is starving, there should be an upper limit on how much money any one person can have. But this book isn't about those issues.

All *this* book says is that it's not fair for people to get rich—and stay rich—*by defrauding people who are poorer than they are.* As you'll soon see, stealing from the poor—actually, from anybody who isn't rich—has become standard operating procedure in this country. In fact, the US government today functions mostly as a huge Robin-Hood-in-reverse.

But doesn't it help the economy?

It's sometimes argued that corporate welfare benefits society as a whole, by recirculating money back into the economy. Of course, that's also true of welfare for the poor, which benefits landlords, supermarkets, variety stores, etc.

What's more, a lot of welfare programs pay for themselves many times over in future savings on health care, prisons and welfare payments. (Head Start is a perfect example—according to conservative estimates, $1 invested in Head Start saves $3 in future costs to society.)

8

Corporate welfare, on the other hand, tends to finance industries that pollute our air, water and soil, so we end up paying for them twice—with our money and with our health. Subsidizing certain businesses or industries is not only unfair to competitors who aren't subsidized, but it also stifles the incentive of the subsidized businesses to innovate and to develop new products, which ultimately makes them less competitive.

Welfare for the rich fosters corruption, both in business and in government. And it's not uncommon for two wealthfare programs to conflict—as when the Interior Department subsidizes irrigation water for agribusinesses and the Agriculture Department pays those same companies not to grow crops with that water. (What do the companies do? Why, sell the water back to local governments at a profit, of course. What else?)

It's not as if the money currently used for wealthfare would suddenly evaporate if we weren't handing it over to the rich. It could go into the economy some other way, and would almost certainly have a more beneficial effect. (For more on this, see the section called *What about the jobs we'd lose?* It starts on p. 25, in the chapter on military waste and fraud.)

There's one final cost to all this wealthfare chicanery. The creative talents of a lot of very bright lawyers, accountants and financial advisors are spent figuring out how to squeeze the maximum benefit out of our labyrinthine tax code. If they weren't wasting their time on that, they could be doing something genuinely useful, which would make the economy more productive for all of us.

Who gets taxed?

Back in the 1950s, US corporations paid 31% of the federal government's general revenues. Today, they pay just 11%. If businesses paid taxes at the same rate they did 40 years ago, the federal deficit would disappear overnight—and that's without eliminating a single direct subsidy or handout.

It's easy for "fiscally responsible" candidates to achieve their dearest goal, balancing the budget. All they have to do is get corporations to pay as much in taxes as they did when what was good for General Motors was good for the country.

Taxes that corporations don't pay have to be raised by taxing individuals. Not by taxing all individuals *indiscriminately*, of course—that would be un-American. A series of tax "reforms" that began in 1977 have cut the rate paid by the richest Americans nearly in half, while Social Security taxes—which are paid overwhelmingly by ordinary wage earners (and not paid at all on income over $62,700)—have steadily risen.

The rich get richer

Not surprisingly, these tax changes have contributed to a widening gap between rich and poor. Between 1983 and 1989, *99%* of the increase in Americans' wealth went to the top 20% of the population, and 62% of it went to

10

the top 1% of the population (currently made up of families whose net worth is $2.35 million or more). Income disparity in the United States is now the widest it's been since the crash of 1929, and it continues to grow.

The total net worth of that top 1% is now equal to the total net worth of the bottom *90%* of the population! In other words, the 2.7 million Americans who are worth $2.35 million or more have as much money as the 240 million Americans who are worth $346,000 or less.

Wherever you look on the economic ladder, the rich are getting richer. The wealth of the top 20% has increased while the wealth of the bottom 80% has decreased. Within that top 20%, the top 5% have gotten richer than the bottom 15%. Within that top 5%, the top 1% have gotten richer than the bottom 4%. Within that top 1%, the top $\frac{1}{4}$% have gotten richer than the bottom $\frac{3}{4}$%.

And so it goes, right up to the 400 wealthiest Americans. In the eight years from 1980 to 1987, their average net worth *tripled.*

Now, we hate paying taxes as much as anybody else, and we're certainly not fans of the IRS. But since corporations and wealthy individuals derive most of the benefit from what the government does, we think they should at least pay their fair share of taxes. They're always blathering on about free enterprise—a mythical system they wouldn't survive in for five minutes if it did exist—so let's assume they mean what they say, and take them off the dole.

Handouts vs. loopholes

Welfare for the rich takes two basic forms—direct subsidies and tax breaks. The latter are more insidious, for two reasons. Unlike subsidies, which typically have to be appropriated by Congress and signed into law by the president each year, tax breaks usually get little scrutiny, and they last until they're repealed by some future tax law.

Subsidies are usually for fixed amounts of money, while the amount the government loses on a loophole depends on how many taxpayers take advantage of it each year, and to what extent. This means tax breaks are basically open-ended—there's no way the government can control, or even accurately predict, what they're going to cost. (Despite these differences, we've lumped subsidies and tax breaks together in each chapter.)

How this book is organized

We've started with the biggest wealthfare and worked our way down to the smallest (which isn't all that small). That way, if you don't make it all the way through the book, you'll still have covered the most important rip-offs and scams. (But then you'll miss some of the most extraordinary ones; for an example, see the section on horse write-offs, which begins on page 118.)

Even in election years, few politicians pay more than lip service to ending corporate welfare (this isn't surprising, considering who finances their campaigns). Current plans to balance the federal budget by 2002 propose cuts to social welfare programs ten times larger than the cuts proposed for corporate welfare.

Though some politicians seem to be working sincerely to limit welfare for the rich, it would be foolish to depend on them. Fortunately, there are plenty of ways ordinary citizens can force changes. For some ideas on how to start, see the chapter entitled *What you can do about all this* (p. 129).

If you run across terms you're not sure of—*median*, say, or *constant dollars*, or *general fund revenues*—consult the glossary that begins on p. 146. (It can also help you appreciate the full significance of terms you *do* know the meaning of, like *billion* and *trillion*.)

If you think something we're saying just *can't* be true—a reaction we've had several times ourselves—you'll find backup for it in *Where we got our facts* (p. 162).

If you still have the stomach for more tales of greed and corruption, check out *Recommended reading* (p. 140) and *Other books in the Real Story series* (p. 192).

And now—into the mire.

MILITARY WASTE AND FRAUD

$172 BILLION A YEAR

When it comes to wasting money, the Pentagon has no peer. For one thing, there's the simple question of scale. For fiscal year 1996, the Pentagon budget was $265 billion ($7 billion more than it requested). That's 5% of our gross national product, a larger percentage than in virtually any other industrialized nation.

In absolute dollars (not as a percentage of GNP), the Pentagon shells out four times more than Russia (the next largest military spender), almost five times more than Japan, six times more than France, over seven times more than Britain or Germany.

Our military budget is the size of the next *six* largest military budgets combined, and it's seventeen times larger than the combined military budgets of all of our "regional adversaries"—Cuba, Syria, Iran, Iraq, North Korea and Libya. It accounts for 37% of all military spending on the planet (in comparison, our economy is only 22% of the world total).

As enormous as the Pentagon's budget is, there's more military spending buried elsewhere—in the Department of Energy's production of fuel for nuclear weapons, in the military portion of the NASA budget, in the VA, etc. By adding in these hidden military expenses, the Center for Defense Information (CDI), a Washington think tank run by retired generals and admirals, concluded that we spend a total of $327 billion a year on the military. (When it did similar computations independently, the War Resisters League came up with $329 billion.)

But that doesn't include what we have to pay for *past* Pentagon budgets. The CDI went back to 1941 and multiplied the military's percentage of each year's budget by the deficit for that year. Using that method, they figured that interest on past military spending cost us $167 billion in fiscal 1996. (The War Resisters League went all the way back to 1789 and came up with $291 billion.)

Since the CDI's estimates are lower, let's be conservative and use them. Adding them together gives us a figure for total military spending—past and present—of $494 billion a year ($9½ billion a week, $1⅓ billion a day).

Waste beyond your wildest dreams

But just the scale of the Pentagon's budget alone can't explain its prodigious ability to waste money. Another quality is required—world-class incompetence. There are so many examples of this that they tend to blur together, numbing the mind. Here are just a few:

According to a US Senate hearing, $13 billion the Pentagon handed out to weapons contractors between 1985 and 1995 was simply "lost." Another $15 billion remains unaccounted for because of "financial management troubles." That's *$28 billion*—right off the top—that has simply *disappeared*. (This is one of those places where we can hardly believe what we're writing. But it's true.)

In the *New York Times*, Anthony Lewis described the amount of Pentagon waste as "literally incalculable. That is because financial managers in the Defense Department cannot produce auditable books. The director of its accounting service so testified to a congressional committee in November." As Colman McCarthy commented in the *National*

Catholic Reporter, "the money might as well have been thrown out of airplanes for all anyone knew where it went."

According to the General Accounting Office (GAO), *80%* of the Navy's purchase orders are inaccurate. An Air Force purchase of $888,000 in ammunition was listed as $333 *million*—an increase of 37,500%. In 1992 alone, the Army Corps of Engineers "lost" $1.3 billion worth of equipment.

But let's not sweat a few billion dollars here and there—the way the Pentagon *really* wastes money is by overpaying contractors. Our reference on that subject is a wonderful book called *The Pentagon Catalog*, by Christopher Cerf and Henry Beard.

This book was the greatest bargain in history. To quote its cover copy: "Buy this catalog for only $4.95 and get this $2,043 nut for *free.*" Attached to each book was a small metal nut, the kind that costs a few cents at the hardware store—and that McDonnell Douglas sold to the Navy for $2,043 each.

Here are some other examples of your tax dollars at work:

- a plain metal bolt from Grumman Aerospace for $898 (a bargain compared to the nut)

- a pair of duckbill pliers Boeing originally proposed charging $2,548 for, but whose price the Air Force *slashed* to $748

- a $469 box wrench, $437 tape measure, $435 hammer, $265 set of screwdrivers and $243 pair of Vise-Grip pliers (all from Gould Simulation Systems)

- a half-inch socket for $504, and a $660 ashtray (both from Grumman)

- a coffee-maker Weber Aircraft charged $7,622 for—but, in fairness, it *was* designed to handle a 100° drop in room temperature or 40 g's of acceleration (we don't know about you, but the first thing we want after being frozen solid or turned into a blob of jelly is a nice, hot cup of coffee)

- a $670 armrest pad from Burns Aerostat

- a toilet seat for which Lockheed charged $640

- a $214 flashlight from Grimes Manufacturing

- our personal favorite: a plastic cap that goes over the end of a stool leg—special price from Boeing: just $1,118 each

We should point out that, for several of these items, the government eventually did negotiate a refund...of about 10%. And while exorbitant prices like these are fairly common, the Pentagon usually pays much less for the products it buys—only about 30% to 50% more than normal commercial prices.

For our final examples, let's turn to the VA (formerly the Veterans Administration, it's now the Department of Veterans Affairs, but everybody still calls it the VA). Because the number of veterans declined from 28 million in 1980 to 23 million in 1995, the VA's hospital system is currently underused. In spite of that, the VA has been spending $560 million a year on new hospitals.

The VA is building a $211-million hospital in northern California, even though three others in the region are operating below capacity.

It's spending $104 million for a new 105-bed wing in Honolulu—even though 63 beds in the same facility were eliminated because they were underused.

Auditors found that thirteen of the surgeons on staff at one VA hospital in southern California—whose salaries averaged $135,000 a year—had performed no surgery *at all* in the prior three months. Nationwide, the VA has 500 more surgeons than it needs; their salaries total $67 million a year.

Career criminals
Take one bloated budget. Add the most incompetent bureaucrats on earth. Only two more ingredients are needed: greed and guile.

For every $640 toilet seat the Pentagon buys, there's some unctuous predator *selling it* for $640. Actually, "unctuous predator" is far too kind. Most military suppliers are—plain and simple—criminals.

According to the *Bulletin of the Atomic Scientists,* every single one of the top ten weapons contractors was convicted of or admitted to defrauding the government between 1980 and 1992. For example:

- Grumman paid the government $20 million to escape criminal liability for coercing subcontractors into making political contributions.

- Lockheed was convicted of paying millions in bribes to obtain classified planning documents.

- Northrop was fined $17 million for falsifying test data on its cruise missiles and fighter jets.

- Rockwell was fined $5.5 million for committing criminal fraud against the Air Force.

In another study, the Project on Government Oversight (PGO) searched public records from October 1989 to February 1994 and found—in just that 4⅓-year period—85 instances of fraud, waste and abuse in weapons contracting. For example:

- Boeing, Grumman, Hughes, Raytheon and RCA pleaded guilty to illegal trafficking in classified documents and paid a total of almost $15 million in restitution, reimbursements, fines, etc.

- Hughes pleaded guilty to procurement fraud in one case, was convicted of it in a second case and, along with McDonnell Douglas and General Motors, settled out-of-court for a total of more than $1 million dollars in a third case.

- Teledyne paid $5 million in a civil settlement for false testing, plus $5 million for repairs.

- McDonnell Douglas settled for a total of more than $22 million in four "defective pricing" cases.

But General Electric was the champ. PGO lists *fourteen* cases, including a conviction for mail and procurement fraud that resulted in a criminal fine of $10 million and restituiton of $2.2 million. In our own research, we found several other examples of GE crimes and civil violations:

- In 1961, GE pleaded guilty to price-fixing and paid a $372,500 fine.

- In 1977, it was convicted of price-fixing again.

- In 1979, it settled out-of-court when the State of Alabama sued it for dumping PCBs in a river.

- In 1981, it was convicted of setting up a $1.25-million slush fund to bribe Puerto Rican officials.
- In 1985, GE pleaded guilty to 108 counts of fraud on a Minuteman missile contract. In addition, the chief engineer of GE's space systems division was convicted of perjury, and GE paid a fine of a million dollars.
- In 1985, it pleaded guilty to falsifying time cards.
- In 1989, it paid the government $3.5 million to settle five civil lawsuits alleging contractor fraud at a jet-engine plant (which involved the alteration of 9,000 daily labor vouchers to inflate its Pentagon billings).
- In 1990, GE was convicted of criminal fraud for cheating the Army on a contract for battlefield computers; it declined to appeal and paid $16 million in criminal and civil fines. ($11.7 million of this amount was to settle government complaints that it had padded its bids on 200 other military and space contracts—which comes to just $58,000 or so per contract.)

In 1993, GE sold its weapons division to Martin Marietta for $3 billion (retaining 23.5% of the stock and two seats on the board of directors).

The largest investigation of Pentagon fraud took place between 1986 and 1990. Called Operation Ill Wind, it began when Pentagon official John Marlowe was caught molesting little girls. He cut a deal to stay out of jail and, for the next few years, secretly recorded hundreds of conversations with weapons contractors.

There's no way of knowing how much the crimes Ill Wind looked into cost the taxpayers, but the investigation, which cost $20 million, brought in ten times that much in fines. According to *Wall Street Journal* reporter Andy Pasztor, "more than 90 companies and individuals were convicted of felonies... including eight of the military's fifteen largest suppliers....Boeing, GE and United Technologies pleaded guilty...Hughes, Unisys, Raytheon, Loral, Litton, Teledyne, Cubic, Hazeltine, Whittaker and LTV...admitted they violated the law."

Unisys signed the largest Pentagon fraud settlement in history: $190 million in fines, penalties and forgone profits (which means they weren't allowed to charge for cost overruns the way military contractors usually do).

Assistant Navy Secretary Melvyn Paisley was the central figure in the Ill Wind scandal and the highest-ranking person convicted (he was sentenced to four years in prison). He ran his office like a supermarket for weapons manufacturers, soaking up bribes, divvying up multibillion-dollar contracts and diverting work to a firm he secretly controlled with a partner.

Paisley may have been a bit more...flamboyant than most, but there was nothing terribly unusual about his approach. As of 1994, nearly 70 of the Pentagon's 100 largest suppliers were under investigation. Fines for that year totaled a record $1.2 billion.

That may sound like a lot, but it's less than 2% of the weapons industry's net income (which averaged $64 billion a year in 1994 and 1995). A billion or two in fines is hardly an incentive to end the corruption and waste in Pentagon contracting.

The black budget

Not all Pentagon waste is visible. Hidden within the military budget is a secret "black budget" that's not subject to any congressional oversight (toothless as that usually is). It includes money for the CIA (tucked away in the Air Force budget, it gets about 10% of the total) and for less well-known but better-funded "intelligence" organizations like the National Security Agency (NSA) and the National Reconnaissance Office (NRO).

In 1995, several members of Congress tried to argue that, with the Cold War over, there was no harm in publishing the total amount of the intelligence black budget, without details on how it was spent. Even this modest proposal went down to defeat but, in the process, led to the absurd spectacle of legislators mentioning the figure—$28 billion for fiscal 1996—while arguing that it shouldn't be publicly disclosed.

John Pike of the Federation of American Scientists estimates that the 1996 black budget included an additional $3 billion or so in military "stealth" projects, for a total of about $31 billion—down from about $36 billion a year during the Reagan years. Pike attributes the decrease to a couple of projects that grew too huge to be hidden in the black budget.

One of the projects that "surfaced" into the public budget is the B-2 bomber. Originally projected to cost $550 million each, B-2's ended up costing $2.2 billion each—literally more than their weight in gold.

Another is MILSTAR, which is designed to "fight and win a six-month nuclear war...long after the White House and the Pentagon are reduced to rubble." The Air Force has tried to kill this idiotic program four times since it emerged from the black budget, but Congress won't listen. MILSTAR has cost us between $8 and $12 billion so far, and could cost another $4.5 billion between 1996 and 2000.

Since the black budget is completely off the books, it encourages waste on a titanic scale. As one Pentagon employee put it: "In a black project, people don't worry about money. If you need money, you got it. If you screw up and need more, you got it. You're just pouring money into the thing until you get it right. The incentive isn't there to do it right the first time. Who's going to question it?"

Well, the founding fathers would have, since the Constitution states that "no money shall be drawn from the Treasury, but in consequence of appropriations made by law" and requires that the government publish a "regular statement...of the receipts and expenditures of all public money." Unfortunately, in 1974 the Supreme Court ruled that if we don't like the black budget, our only recourse is to elect politicians who won't allow it. (Or we could get better people on the Supreme Court.)

Don't call it bribery

Why do our legislators put up with military waste and fraud? For the same reason they do anything. Defense PACs gave members of

Congress $7.5 million in 1993 and 1994. And PAC money is just part of the story.

Of the $4.5 billion in unrequested weapons funding added to the Pentagon budget for fiscal 1996, 74% was spent in or near the home districts of representatives who sit on the House National Security Committee. Another $290 million was spent in or around Newt Gingrich's home district, Cobb County, Georgia. (Cobb gets more federal pork than any county except Arlington in Virginia, which is right next to Washington, and Brevard in Florida, where Cape Canaveral is located.)

Although the Pentagon insists that it doesn't need any more B-2 bombers, Norman Dicks (D–Washington) and Ted Stevens (R–Alaska) don't care. Dicks—who's one of the largest recipients of military PAC money in the House—received over $10,000 from nine major B-2 contractors in the four months just before the battle to resurrect B-2 funding. Stevens got $37,000 between 1989 and 1994, making him one of the top ten recipients of PAC contributions from B-2 contractors. (Isn't it amazing how little politicians cost?)

If PAC money isn't enough, military lobbyists can always argue jobs. It didn't hurt funding for the B-2 that spending for it was spread across 88% of all congressional districts and all but two states.

Liberal California Representative Maxine Waters defended her vote to continue B-2 funding by candidly admitting that it was one of the few ways she knew to bring federal jobs to her district. (Since her district is

South-Central Los Angeles, you can understand her desperation.)

There's no conceivable need for Seawolf submarines (which cost $2.4 billion apiece)—except for the votes in Connecticut, where it's built, and in surrounding states. That's why liberal New England senators like Ted Kennedy, John Kerry and George Mitchell supported it, as did Bill Clinton—who needed votes from those states—in his 1992 campaign.

Neither the Air Force nor the Navy wants any part of the V-22 Osprey assault plane, which the Bush administration tried in vain to kill. But it's supported by legislators in Texas and Pennsylvania—the two states that do the most contracting for it—and by Clinton, who...oh, you get the idea.

What about the jobs we'd lose?

If new weapons systems are nothing more than make-work programs, they're really inefficient ones. A 1992 Congressional study estimated that shifting money from the Pentagon to state and local governments would create two jobs for every one it eliminates. Building weapons we don't need is so wasteful that the economy would probably be better off if we just paid people the same money to stay at home.

The Congressional Budget Office concluded that a billion dollars spent on successfully promoting arms exports creates 25,000 jobs, but if that same billion is spent on mass transit, it creates 30,000 jobs; on housing, 36,000 jobs; on education, 41,000 jobs; or on health care, 47,000 jobs.

Aside from the cost, using federal money to prop up military contractors creates a disincentive for them to convert to civilian products. Shifting Pentagon funds to urgently needed domestic uses would be good for both the US and the rest of the world. As President Eisenhower put it, "Every gun that is made, every warship launched, every rocket fired signifies, in the final sense, a theft from those who hunger and are not fed, those who are cold and not clothed."

Pentagon boosters argue that military spending has already been slashed too far, since more than 800,000 military-related jobs have disappeared since 1990. But many of these layoffs were in nonmilitary divisions of the companies, and more than half of them were caused by the economy contracting in a recession, not by smaller Pentagon budgets—especially since they've dropped off only slightly from their all-time high of $304 billion (adjusted for inflation) in 1989.

Just eight companies—McDonnell Douglas, Lockheed, Martin Marietta, Boeing, General Dynamics, Northrop Grumman, Raytheon and Hughes—were responsible for half of all military contractors' layoffs in 1993. Only 15% of Boeing's layoffs and a third of McDonnell Douglas' were related to military production. After the firings, the stocks of these eight companies rose by 20% to 140%, and the salaries of their CEOs soared.

The revolving door
Another reason for Pentagon waste and fraud is the revolving door between military con-

tractors and government personnel. Before he was Secretary of Defense, Caspar Weinberger was a top executive at Bechtel, which does massive engineering projects for the Pentagon and foreign clients like Saudi Arabia. Before he was Secretary of State, George Shultz was president of Bechtel.

Before his days as a Navy felon, Melvyn Paisley worked for Boeing—as did his boss at the Pentagon, Navy Secretary John Lehman. Secretary of Defense William Perry and CIA Director John Deutch both did consulting work for Martin Marietta before they joined the Clinton administration. The list goes on and on.

Generals have an interest in keeping weapons contractors happy—at least if they want to sit on the boards of corporations after they retire. Contractors can use their connections at the Pentagon to find work there and, like Paisley, feed lucrative contracts to their friends in the private sector.

On both sides of the revolving door, militarists live in the lap of luxury. Nobody batted an eyelash when Paisley entertained contractors in staterooms on the Queen Elizabeth, nor is there ever much dismay when military aircraft are used, at a cost of tens of thousands of dollars an hour, to fly politicians, lobbyists and weapons contractors on pleasure trips.

Direct handouts

Still, personal perks don't cost us much compared to *corporate* perks. For example, when Lockheed and Martin Marietta merged to become Lockheed Martin, $92 million in bonuses—or "triggered compensation," as they prefer to call it—was handed out to top executives and members of the board. They expect the government to pick up $31 million of that.

John Deutch quietly reversed a 40-year ban on such compensation when he was at the Pentagon. The biggest bonus, $8.2 million, went to the new company's president, Norman Augustine, who Deutch and William Perry had done work for at Martin Marietta.

Both Deutch and Perry obtained waivers from an ethics regulation that prohibits Pentagon officials from dealing with people they formerly did business with until a year has passed. (Up to 30,000 employees will lose their jobs as a result of this merger.)

Military contractors milk the government in other ways as well. It's common for the State Department to give foreign aid to brutal dictatorships like Indonesia and Guatemala, with the requirement that the money be used to buy US weapons. Each year this program results in the transfer of $5–7 billion from US taxpayers to US arms merchants (not to mention the murder of lots of innocent people in the countries involved).

The Pentagon has similar programs that not only provide subsidies to foreign countries to buy from US weapons suppliers but also help them negotiate the sale. In 1994, General Dynamics and Lockheed received a total of $1.9 billion in foreign military sales awards—126,567% more than the $1.5 million they gave to candidates for federal offices in the

1994 elections. (As we've already remarked, politicians sure are a bargain.)

Thanks in large part to these Pentagon programs—on which we spend $5.4 billion a year, almost half our total foreign aid expenditure—the US is the largest arms supplier on earth, with 43% of the world trade. What's more, many of these loans are ultimately defaulted on or forgiven. Egypt, for example, was let off the hook for $7 billion in loans, as a reward for participating in the Gulf War.

Selling the story to the public

It's clear why politicians, military contractors and Pentagon bureaucrats support the Pentagon system. But how do they sell it to the rest of us, who are harmed by it?

After World War II, President Truman faced the same problem—how to keep the war industries going without a war to justify them. Senator Arthur Vandenburg of Michigan supplied the answer: "Scare the hell out of the American people."

For the next forty years, the Soviet Union was used for this purpose. There was just one hitch—the USSR's military capabilities were always significantly inferior to ours. Ah, that's where the guile comes in.

First there was the "bomber gap." In 1955, Air Force intelligence warned that the USSR would have between 500 and 800 intercontinental bombers within five years. At the time, the US had over 1000 such bombers; the Soviets had fewer than 40, and never built more than 200.

Then there was the "missile gap." Introduced in 1957, it warned that the Soviets "could" have 3000 ICBMs (intercontinental ballistic missiles) by 1960. Apparently the Soviets decided not to bother, since by 1960, they had a grand total of *four* ICBMs. Still, the "missile gap" served its real purpose, which was to generate billions of dollars in military spending.

Military expert Seymour Melman identified seven other fictitious "gaps" in our defenses that were used to scare the hell out of the American people: the antiballistic missile gap, the fighter gap, the megatonnage gap, the submarine gap, the survivability gap, the strategy gap and the security gap. And then there was the "window of vulnerability" that Reagan used to justify his $1.5-*trillion* increase in military spending, which helped turn us from the world's largest creditor nation to the world's largest debtor nation.

The Strategic Defense Initiative—better known as SDI or Star Wars—is another example. It's extremely expensive, counters a "threat" that's virtually nonexistent, and almost certainly will never work. (Missile experts are fond of saying that SDI is like trying to deflect a bullet that's coming at you by hitting it with another bullet.)

The Pentagon admits to faking the results of Star Wars tests it ran in 1984. They said they did it to deceive the Soviets, but of course they also deceived the media and Congress, which poured more money into this useless boondoggle. Between 1983 and 1993, more than

$35 billion was spent on Star Wars, with basically nothing to show for it.

In one of the weasel-fests Bill Clinton has become famous for, he announced he was killing Star Wars. Only later did the story come out in the alternative press that SDI wasn't actually dead—it had just been *renamed* the Ballistic Missile Defense Organization.

Removed from public debate, minimal attention was paid to SDI—er, BMDO—until the GOP decided they wanted to give it *more* money. (It's currently funded at $3.8 billion a year.)

All this nonsense has succeeded in denying us the "peace dividend" we were promised at the end of the Cold War. Even though the Soviet system has completely collapsed, the Pentagon's budget is only 7% lower (adjusted for inflation) than the Cold War average, and it's 50% higher than it was in 1980, before the Reagan buildup began.

In its desperate attempt to keep spending levels up, the Pentagon has been auditioning new enemies; Arab terrorists and drug dealers have been two of the most popular. Then the movie *Independence Day* introduced a new possibility—extraterrestrials! They come from other worlds, seeking our "resources." (Of course, if they have the technology to cross interstellar space, they're not going to need our "resources"—or anybody else's—but that's just one idiotic premise out of thousands in this puerile ad for military hardware.)

Appealing as the extraterrestrial scenario is, the Pentagon would prefer something a little more down-to-earth. So they've come up with the most paranoid worst-case scenario they could think of.

According to their "two-war plan," we're supposed to be in grave danger unless we can simultaneously engage in two conflicts, each the size of the Gulf War, in different parts of the world, completely by ourselves.

Why wouldn't we get any help from our allies? Why couldn't we put one war on hold—with heavy bombing, say—until we won the other one? The answer's obvious: because then there'd be no way to justify a gargantuan military budget.

How much military spending is waste?

Even if you accept the absurd two-war plan, lots of savings are still possible:

- We have more Trident missiles than we could ever use, and nobody to aim them at. But the Navy isn't happy with their old Tridents (currently funded at $787 million a year). They want to replace them with a newer version, even though both kinds of Tridents are likely to be eliminated under the next arms-control agreement, START III.

- Although our 121 C-5 and 265 C-144 transport planes are perfectly adequate, the Pentagon wants to replace a bunch of them with 120 new C-17s, at a total cost of $45 billion.

- The rationale for the F-22 fighter is especially weak. It was designed to achieve air superiority in the 1990s over the now-defunct Soviet Union. We already have 900 F-15s (which the GAO calls the best tactical aircraft in the world), and none of our real or potential enemies have more than a handful of planes that come anywhere close to matching its capabilities. That hasn't stopped the Pentagon from asking for 442 F-22s, at a total cost of $72 billion.

- Even a hawk like Barry Goldwater points out the waste involved in the Army, Navy, Air Force and Marines each having its own air force. Both the Marines and the Army have light infantry divisions, and the Navy and the Air Force aren't satisfied with the same kind of satellites and cruise missiles—each has to have its own kind.

- The Pentagon keeps 100,000 troops in Europe and 70,000 in Korea and Japan. We spend $80 billion a year on NATO, $59 billion a year in South Korea and $48 billion a year in the Persian Gulf. In all of these cases, the countries we're supposedly defending have militaries that are better-equipped and much better-funded than their enemies'.

- As we've mentioned above, even the Pentagon doesn't want any more B-2 bombers, V-22 Osprey assault planes or additional Star Wars funds. The Navy doesn't want the Seawolf submarine and admits it doesn't need another $3.5-billion nuclear-powered aircraft carrier. But try telling that to the companies that make those weapons, or to the politicians whose campaigns they fund.

By now it should be obvious that the "defense" budget isn't based on any rational calculation of what the defense of this country actually requires—it's based on what US arms manufacturers can get away with (almost anything, it turns out).

Attaching the word "defense" to this spending isn't just misleading—it's the complete opposite of the truth, since military waste and fraud make our country weaker, not stronger. The preposterously obese Pentagon budget is the single greatest threat there is to our national security.

It's not just wild-eyed radicals who feel this way:

- Lawrence Korb, a military planner under Reagan who's now with the Brookings Institution, says we could have the most overwhelmingly powerful military in the world for around $150 billion a year.

- In a report called *Ending Overkill*, the *Bulletin of the Atomic Scientists* laid out a detailed military budget that includes funding for a lot of programs we think are unnecessary (Star Wars, for example). Even so, its report calls for scaling down the military budget to $115 billion by the year 2000, and states that this would still give us a force "adequate to undertake six or eight Somalia-like operations at the same time, or to mount a force somewhat larger than the American part of Desert Storm."

- The Center for Defense Information (founded, as we mentioned earlier, by retired generals and admirals) thinks we could get by quite nicely with about a million soldiers, instead of the 1.4 million we now have, and with a Pentagon budget of "about $200 billion."

The average of those three estimates is $155 billion a year—quite a bit less than the $327 billion a year we actually spend. (And remember: that $327 billion doesn't include the $167 billion or more we lay out each year to service debt that's the result of past military programs. Unfortunately, there isn't much we can do about that past debt—except to cut down on present military budgets, so the problem doesn't keep getting worse.)

Subtracting $155 billion from $327 billion gives us a figure for *current* military waste and fraud of $172 billion a year—almost $500 million a day—virtually all of which goes to large corporations and super-rich individuals. (Sure, some of it pays for ordinary people's salaries, but they'd also be earning money if they were doing something useful.) Half a billion dollars a day could buy a lot of medical care, or fill a lot of potholes, or...you name it. After all, it's your money.

SOCIAL SECURITY TAX INEQUITIES

$53 BILLION A YEAR

You remember Ronald Reagan, don't you? He was elected president in 1980 on a promise to cut taxes. ("When they insist we can't reduce taxes...and balance the budget too, one six-word answer will do: *Yes we can, and yes we will.*" Of course that's *seven* words, but that's closer than he usually came.)

Reagan did reduce taxes...for the rich. For everybody else, he signed the largest tax increase in US history (adjusted for inflation), which far exceeded his tax cuts. How did he manage that? By raising Social Security tax rates while he lowered income tax rates.

Social Security tax is a major technique for transferring the tax burden away from the rich. One reason is that it only applies to "earned" income; income from investments is exempt. Another reason is that there's a ceiling—currently $62,700—on how much earned income is taxed.

Anyone who earns $62,700 or more pays the same Social Security tax Bill Gates does—needless to say, it amounts to a slightly higher percentage of their income. This makes Social Security one of our most regressive taxes. A family that made the (1993) median income of $37,800 paid 7.65% of its income in Social Security tax, while one that made ten times as much paid 1.46% and one that made a hundred times as much paid 0.1% (one-tenth of 1%).

Between 1971 and 1991, families making the median income saw their combined Social Security and income taxes go up 329%, while the combined tax bill of families making more than $1 million a year dropped 34%. As a result, most working people today pay more Social Security tax than they do income tax.

But the trust fund was just sitting there

The Social Security tax has been raised nine times since 1977. Because these massive tax hikes were sold to the public as a way of saving Social Security, one of the government's most popular programs, both parties supported them, without much controversy or publicity.

People have been told that the trust fund has to begin racking up huge surpluses or it will go bankrupt when the Baby Boom generation begins to retire. (Since the Baby Boom lasted from 1946 to 1964, the first boomers will start collecting Social Security in 2008, at age 62.)

The extra money doesn't just sit in the trust fund; the government borrows it to pay for other things, like military waste and corporate welfare—making Social Security tax, in effect, just another form of income tax. Over a *trillion* dollars, plus interest, will have to be repaid in order for Social Security, and other trust funds like Medicare, to meet their obligations in the next century. Can you guess who's going to repay it?

The government borrows money from itself to disguise the fact that it's spending more than it takes in. This shell game has been around for almost 30 years. Back when government was more honest, Social Security's income and expenditures were treated as separate from the discretionary part of the federal budget (the part the government could spend as it wished). The trust fund took in money and paid out benefits, and it wasn't included in the budgets passed by Congress and signed by the President.

But in 1969, the so-called "unified budget" was instituted. By combining Social Security with other taxes, President Johnson could claim that the US was running a surplus, even though it was actually being bled dry by the Vietnam War. To this day, the unified budget makes military spending look like a smaller percentage of discretionary federal spending than it really is.

Through the ceiling

Social Security tax receipts for fiscal 1996 are estimated at $426 billion, and outlays at $357 billion. If the wealthy had to pay Social Security tax on *all* their earned income, the government would have taken in an additional $53 billion.

In other words, if there were no ceiling, Social Security taxes could be *reduced* by $53 billion (assuming Social Security benefits stayed the same). That doesn't include investment income, *all* of which is exempt from Social Security tax, but let's be conservative and use $53 billion as our total for this category.

ACCELERATED DEPRECIATION

$37 BILLION A YEAR

In 1971, the Nixon administration issued an executive order allowing, for the first time, *accelerated depreciation*—that is, writing off the costs of equipment and buildings faster than they actually wear out. This led to a massive decline in corporate tax payments.

When the write-off was expanded in Reagan's 1981 tax plan, an even more massive decline occurred: by 1983, the percentage of total federal tax revenues paid by corporations was half of what it had been just three years earlier.

Of the 250 largest and most profitable companies in the US, a quarter—whose pretax profits totalled $50 billion—paid no federal income tax at all between 1981 and 1983, and half of them didn't pay in one or more of those three years.

The 1986 tax reform disallowed the accelerated depreciation of real estate, but left the loophole for machinery and other equipment. So the accelerated depreciation scam is still with us, and costs us an average of $37 billion a year.

A company can even generate a negative tax rate by buying equipment and leasing it to another company, in return for tax deductions the other company can't use. (Being able to trade deductions and credits is a leftover from the huge 1981–86 Reagan corporate tax pig-out.)

Company A never sees the equipment, but they accelerate depreciation on it; company B gets to write off the leasing costs. GE was one company that used this strategy; it saved them a billion dollars in taxes between 1986 and 1992. And they weren't the only ones.

Business leaders like to argue that tax breaks like accelerated depreciation stimulate the overall economy. But the evidence runs the other way.

As a former Reagan Treasury official told *Business Week* magazine, "In 1981, manufacturing had its largest tax cut ever and immediately went down the tubes. In 1986, they had their largest tax increase and went gangbusters [on investment]."

In the heyday of accelerated depreciation (1981–86), the economy grew an average of

1.9% a year. After accelerated depreciation was limited (1986–89), the economy grew an average of 2.7% a year.

That's not surprising, since corporate tax savings are seldom used to boost the economy. For example, Westinghouse got a $215-million tax break from accelerated depreciation in 1993; over the next two years, it cut 24,700 jobs. Accelerated depreciation reduced American Brands' 1994 tax bill by $115 million; in gratitude, it laid off 10,780 workers.

There's one final problem with accelerated depreciation: because it's such a gigantic tax break, it distorts business decisions. The tax benefit it confers often outweighs the actual risks and rewards of an investment, and in the long run, that sort of distortion is very bad for the economy.

During the extended wrangling over the federal budget for fiscal 1996, a group of business leaders fired off a stern letter to President Clinton and Congress, urging them to get their act together. Seven signers of the letter were the CEOs of Ford, Exxon, General Motors, Chrysler, IBM, Amoco and Chevron—companies that had each used accelerated depreciation to defer a billion dollars in tax payments. When consumer advocate Ralph Nader asked them if they'd consider forgoing tax loopholes of this kind to help balance the budget, their reply was a stony silence.

In addition to benefiting corporations, accelerated depreciation also helps wealthy individuals (who own most of the stocks and bonds the corporations issue). On average, tax breaks from accelerated depreciation are worth more than $13,000 a year to households making over $200,000, but less than $70 a year to households earning under $50,000.

LOWER TAXES ON CAPITAL GAINS

$37 BILLION A YEAR
(NOT COUNTING HOME SALES)

The larger someone's income is, the larger the portion of it (on average) that comes from investments rather than a salary. Some investment income takes the form of dividends and interest, but a major part of it is *capital gains*—profits made from the sale of assets like stocks, bonds and real estate whose value went up while the investor owned them.

People who aren't rich sometimes have capital gains too—when they sell houses that have appreciated in value, for example—but less than 8% of all capital gains income goes to people who make $50,000 a year or less (three-quarters of all taxpayers). 69% goes to people making over $100,000 a year, 40% to those making over $500,000, and 32% to those making a million dollars a year or more (about one person in 6600).

As Citizens for Tax Justice put it, "more than any other kind of income, capital gains are concentrated at the very top of the income scale." *97%* of the benefit from the 1993 capital gains tax cut went to the richest 1% of the population. But that's not enough for them—they want to pay nothing. Thus the "flat tax" plans of Dick Armey and Steve Forbes exempt capital gains from taxation completely!

Two kinds of taxes—low or no

One of the slick things about capital gains (for those who have them) is that they aren't taxed until the asset is sold. But you can still *cash in* on them in the meantime—all you have to do is borrow money, using the appreciated value of the asset as collateral. (You do have to pay interest on the loan, of course, but interest on business loans is tax-deductible.)

When capital gains *are* taxed, they get special treatment. For the 65 years from 1921 to 1986, the capital gains rate was lower—often enormously lower—than the rate for salaries and other "ordinary income." The 1986 tax reform bill made the rates the same, but that radical idea was eliminated in the tax "reform" bill of 1990, and the 1993 tax "reform" bill cut the capital gains rate even further. As of this writing, it's capped at 28%, while the top rate for ordinary income is 39.6% (39% for corporations).

In addition to the basic unfairness of penalizing people for working (by taxing earned income at a higher rate), the tax code is riddled with exceptions and special treatment for various groups. For example, coal, timber, iron ore and certain agricultural enterprises are allowed to cut their tax bill by treating part of their normal business profits as capital gains, rather than as ordinary income.

Certain "small business corporate stocks" get another special break—they can deduct capital losses up to $100,000 from ordinary income (for everyone else, capital losses beyond the first $3,000 can only be offset against capital gains). In 1993, another special exclusion was added—half the capital gains from certain risky ventures (deemed "likely to fail") aren't taxed at all.

Real estate speculators get an especially sweet deal. They can avoid capital gains taxes on appreciated properties *indefinitely,* simply by trading them in what are called *Starker* or *1031 exchanges.* Not until they finally sell a property without buying another do they have to pay capital gains tax on the increased value of all the properties in the chain.

But there's even a way around that. If they keep trading properties until they die, their heirs can sell the property without paying *any* capital gains tax on the accumulated appreciation. And when property is bestowed as a gift, no capital gains tax is due on it until the person receiving the gift sells it.

Low rates are bad for business

As with accelerated depreciation, defenders of a lower capital gains tax rate argue that it encourages greater savings and more investment, which results in more jobs, a higher rate of economic growth and even in higher tax revenues (since the wealthy have less incentive to hide their income in tax shelters).

But by cutting the rate, the government is simply creating a new and better tax shelter, one that's more attractive to the rich than the ones they've been using. And using tax rates to encourage investments that otherwise make little business sense ultimately sabotages economic growth.

The jobs-and-growth argument is even less convincing. As you can see from the chart below, when the top capital gains tax rate goes down, employment and the growth rate of the economy also tend to go *down;* when the capital gains rate goes up, employment and the economy tend to also. That's exactly the opposite of what's predicted by supporters of lower capital gains taxes.

year of change	change in top capital gains rate	change in employment, next two years	change in growth rate, next two years
1976	+3.4%	+1.9%	+1.3%
1978	−11.9%	−1.5%	−5.5%
1981	−8.0%	−2.0%	−2.5%
1987	+8.0%	+1.6%	+1.6%

Now, obviously, other factors than the capital gains rate affect employment and the growth of the economy. But we find it amazing that people can blithely make the argument that lower capital gains taxes mean more jobs and a healthier economy when so much of the evidence goes in the other direction.

The lower tax rate for capital gains isn't a trivial matter. Between 1996 and 2002, it will cost us almost $37 billion a year—and that *doesn't* include capital gains on home sales.

THE S&L BAILOUT

$32 BILLION, EVERY YEAR FOR THIRTY YEARS

The savings and loan industry began over a century ago for the sole purpose of providing home mortgages. Until the 1930s, S&Ls (sometimes called *thrifts*—which is pretty ironic, considering their recent history) got along quite nicely more or less on their own. But when nearly two thousand of them failed during the Great Depression, the government began regulating them in earnest, and providing deposit insurance to quell fears of further S&L failures.

Compared to the greener pastures of the commercial banks, the S&Ls' opportunities for financial chicanery were slight, so there wasn't a great deal of corruption there. The trouble began when Jimmy Carter appointed Paul Volcker chairman of the Federal Reserve Board (commonly called "the Fed") in late 1979.

The Fed is supposed to minimize unemployment as well as inflation, and before 1979, it tried to achieve some sort of balance between the two goals. But under Volcker and his successor, Alan Greenspan, it's simply aimed for low inflation, regardless of the effect that has on jobs. In fact, Greenspan has asked Congress to relieve the Fed of responsibility for keeping unemployment down.

Inflation was high when Volcker took over—13% or so. To get it under control, he tightened the money supply. This brought on a monster recession, the biggest since World War II. Within a year, the prime rate shot up to the unheard-of level of 21.5% (compared to an average of 7.6% for the fourteen previous years). Unemployment peaked at just under 11%.

According to author Robert Sherrill, Volcker stated, upon taking office, that "the standard of living for the average American has to decline." Sherrill says Volcker was recommended by David Rockefeller because "Wall Street and the international banking fraternity loved [Volcker]. They hated inflation—bankers don't like to be repaid in money that is softer than the money they lend, even if the softer money makes the economy hum—and they knew that Volcker was mean enough to destroy the economy to save the hardness of their dollars."

Volcker's policies caused a combination of inflation and recession called "stagflation." This put the squeeze on S&Ls. Most S&L mortgages were fixed-rate, so the S&Ls couldn't raise the interest they charged on those.

But because their depositors were withdrawing money by the billions and placing it in higher-yielding money market funds or government bonds, the S&Ls did have to raise the rates they *paid* on savings accounts and CDs. Finally, because of the recession, homeowners started defaulting on their mortgages in droves, and S&L bankruptcies skyrocketed.

If it is broke, fix it
By the time Ronald Reagan took office in 1981, two-thirds of the nation's S&Ls were

losing money and many were broke. If all the problem thrifts had been shut down right then, the government's insurance fund would have covered their debts.

Instead, the government delayed an average of two years—and, in some cases, as many as seven years—thus allowing bankrupt S&Ls to go on losing billions of dollars. This delay also gave S&Ls a chance to gamble on questionable investments, in an attempt to regain solvency. But first they had to convince Congress to deregulate them.

One night in 1980, Representative Fernand St Germain (D–Rhode Island), whose $10,000-to-$20,000-a-year restaurant and bar tab was paid for by the S&L industry's chief lobbyist, proposed raising federal insurance on S&L savings accounts from $40,000 to $100,000—even though the average size of an S&L account was $6,000. He waited until after midnight, when only eleven representatives were still on the floor of the House; they approved his proposal unanimously.

But St Germain was just getting warmed up. In 1982, he cosponsored a bill that removed all controls on what S&Ls could charge for interest and released them from their century-old reliance on home mortgages.

Around the same time, the Reagan administration ended the requirement that S&Ls lend money only in their own communities, allowed them to offer 100% financing (i.e. no down payments), let real estate developers own their own S&Ls, and permitted S&L owners to lend money to themselves.

These changes were like taping a sign to the S&Ls' backs that read, "Defraud me." In fact, it's widely rumored that Mafia lawyers and accountants carefully monitored the progress of this bill as it worked its way through Congress, ready to pounce the moment it became law.

Scoundrel time

Whatever truth there is to that rumor, the "defraud me" sign worked. J. William Oldenburg bought State Savings of Salt Lake City for $10.5 million, then had it pay him $55 million for a piece of land he'd bought for $874,000.

With the help of a shadowy figure named Herman K. Beebe, who served a year for bank fraud, Don Dixon bought Vernon Savings and Loan—one of the nation's healthiest—then set up a series of corporations for it to loan money to. Four years later, he left Vernon $1.3 billion in debt.

Beebe also had money in Silverado Savings, an S&L partly owned by President Bush's son Neil. Silverado told a prospective borrower he couldn't have $10 million; instead, he should borrow $15 million and buy $5 million in Silverado stock.

Although federal examiners knew Silverado was leaking cash as early as 1985, it wasn't closed down until December 1988, a month after Bush was elected president. Because Silverado kept leaking cash for those three years, it ended up costing taxpayers more than a billion dollars.

Robert Corson, who helped the CIA smuggle and launder money, bought Kleburg County Savings and Loan and bankrupted it in nine months. *Houston Post* reporter Pete Brewton found 24 failed S&Ls with ties to the CIA. One of these was Peoples Savings and Loan in Llano, Texas, which loaned $3 million to Ray Corona, a drug smuggler, and $2.3 million to his associate Harold White.

One of Corona's drug-smuggling associates was Frank Castro, a Cuban exile involved in Oliver North's contra resupply network. Herman Beebe's Palmer National Bank was also involved with North; it loaned money to customers who then channeled it to the Swiss bank accounts used to supply the contras.

The Reagan administration not only failed to police the industry while all this was going on, it dreamt up ways to keep insolvent S&Ls propped up even longer. By 1988, the government was spending a billion dollars a month keeping "zombie thrifts" afloat.

Everyone in the S&L industry and Congress knew that a bailout would be necessary, but a conspiracy of silence kept the issue out of public debate. Democratic presidential candidate Michael Dukakis tried to raise the issue in 1988, but dropped it under pressure from his running mate, Lloyd Bentsen (who had been part-owner of a couple of Texas S&Ls).

They rob—we pay

As we said, if the insolvent S&Ls had been shut down in 1980, the government's insurance fund would have covered the losses and only administrative costs would have been incurred. If they'd been liquidated in May 1985, it would have cost less than $16 billion. By the end of 1985, the costs were estimated at $30 billion.

In 1989, Congress finally came up with $157 billion to bail out the S&Ls. But by that time, the costs were over $200 billion (and they continue to rise to this day). To make up the difference, the Resolution Trust Corporation was formed; it sold off the assets of failed S&Ls, mostly at bargain-basement prices in sweetheart deals.

For example, Robert Bass, one of the richest men in America, bought American Savings and Loan for $350 million, then received $2 *billion* in government subsidies to help him resurrect it. (With that much money, you could probably raise the dead.) During one week in 1988, the government promised $8 billion in assistance to nine S&L purchasers; one of them put $20 million down, and the other eight paid nothing.

That same year, the First Gibraltar Bank was merged with four failing S&Ls and sold to Ronald Perelman (at the time, the fifth richest man in America). Perelman and his partners paid just $315 million for $7.1 billion in good assets; the government then gave them $5.1 billion to cover bad assets, plus $900 million in tax breaks. In the first year Perelman et al. owned it, Gibraltar made a profit of $129 million and got an additional $121 million in tax breaks.

Check, please

The $157-billion bailout was financed by floating 30-year bonds, the interest on which will make the ultimate cost much higher. The actual total will depend on what interest rates end up being between 1990 and 2020, but estimates range from $500 billion to $1.4 trillion (in other words, *1,400 billion dollars!*).

If we could predict interest rates, we'd be vacationing on Jupiter right now, so let's just split the difference between these two estimates and predict that the ultimate cost for the S&L bailout will be $950 billion. That comes to about $32 billion a year—and we're locked into it for thirty years, no matter what we do or who we elect.

All this money will come from taxpayers and will go to the people who bought the bonds. So, ultimately, the S&L bailout amounts to a massive transfer of wealth from ordinary people to investors (most of whom are wealthy)—as well as to the crooks who looted the S&Ls. (Few of them were convicted, by the way, and the average sentence of those who were was less than two years.)

Probably the worst part of the S&L bailout is the message it sends to high-flying con men. It says, "Plunder all you want. As long as your political connections are solid, you'll get to keep the money and probably won't suffer more than a slap on the wrist." (Charles Keating only went to jail because his abuses were so extreme; he was the exception, not the rule.)

The authors of the best book on the S&L scandal, *Inside Job*, conclude that, rather than a lot of mindless blundering, there was "some kind of network...a purposeful and coordinated system of fraud. At each step of our investigation our suspicions grew because, of the dozens of savings and loans we investigated, we never once examined a thrift—no matter how random the choice— without finding someone there we already knew from another failed S&L."

HOMEOWNERS' TAX BREAKS

$26 BILLION A YEAR

Homeowners get five different federal tax breaks that the 40 million American families who rent their homes don't. The best-known of these allows interest paid on mortgages for principal residences and/or vacation homes to be deducted on the federal income tax return.

The mortgage interest deduction
Supporters of this deduction say it's in the public interest to encourage home owner- ship, yet about two-thirds of the benefits go to families with incomes of $75,000 or high- er—who hardly need encouragement to own property. (Canada, which doesn't have such a deduction, has about the same rate of home ownership as the US.)

Although about 63 million US families own their homes, only 27 million—fewer than half—claimed the mortgage interest deduction in 1994. That's probably because it isn't worth it for most nonwealthy taxpayers to itemize their deductions.

What's more, the lower your tax bracket, the less the deduction is worth to you. If a family in the 15% bracket pays $5000 in mortgage interest a year, they save $750 ($5000 x 15%) on their taxes. But if a family in the top tax bracket (39.6%) takes out the same mortgage, the deduction is worth $1980 to them ($5000 x 39.6%)—more than $2\frac{1}{2}$ times as much.

The National Housing Institute calculates that this deduction cost the Treasury slightly more than $58 billion in fiscal 1995, and that half that total—$29 billion—went to people with incomes over $100,000. (In comparison, the entire 1995 budget for HUD—the Department of Housing and Urban Development—was $26 billion.)

According to the Progressive Policy Institute (PPI), only about 5% of home mortgages are over $300,000. By capping the deduction there—with an adjustment for areas with higher-than-average housing costs—we'd save an estimated $4.1 billion a year. Leaving off that adjustment for high-cost areas, a $300,000 cap would save us $6.7 billion a year (according to the Congressional Black Caucus).

Capping the deduction at $250,000—as proposed by former Senator Bob Packwood—would save $7 billion a year and would only affect 1.2 million taxpayers (which means the $300,000 cap would affect even fewer people).

Limiting the deduction to $12,000 in interest payments for single people and $20,000 for couples would save $9.6 billion a year (according to the Concord Coalition).

All these proposals seem to make sense, so let's just take an average of them and say that removing welfare for the rich from the mortgage interest deduction would save us $6.9 billion a year.

Other tax advantages of owning a home
The mortgage interest deduction isn't the only way the law shifts the tax burden to renters. A special, one-time deal exempts homeowners who sell their principal residences after the age of 55 from taxes on the first $125,000 of the profit. According to the White House, this exemption cost the Treasury $5.2 billion in fiscal 1996.

But you don't have to wait until you're 55. If you sell your home and buy another one of equal or greater value within two years before or after the sale, you can defer the tax on whatever profit you made on the first sale. You can keep on trading up like that and never pay capital gains tax, until you finally sell your house without replacing it—or replace it with one that costs less. (If you reach 55 before that happens, $125,000 of your final profits will be tax-free.) The White House estimates this cost us $14.6 billion in fiscal 1996.

Homeowners can also deduct state and local property taxes on their federal income tax returns. According to the White House, this deprives the Treasury of $16.1 billion a year.

Finally, homeowners can deduct the interest paid on home equity loans (which sit on top of the basic mortgage). Let's say you have a mountain of credit-card debt. You take out a home equity loan and use the money to pay off the credit cards. Suddenly your interest payments, which weren't deductible, are. Phasing out this deduction would save another $2.3 billion a year (according to PPI).

Those are the breaks

So, to add everything up: The $125,000 over-55 exemption costs us $5.2 billion a year; the capital gains deferral, $14.6 billion; the property tax deduction, $16.1 billion; and the home equity loan deduction, $2.3 billion.

That comes to $38.2 billion, but not all of it is welfare for the rich. Since about half the mortgage interest deduction goes to people with incomes above $100,000, we can use 50% as a benchmark and divide that $38.2 billion in half. This gives us $19.1 billion.

But that doesn't include the $58 billion mortgage interest deduction itself. We could make an argument for adding the half of it that goes to people with incomes above $100,000, but let's be conservative once again and just count the $6.9 billion a year we lose by not capping it at a reasonable level. That brings us to a total of $26 billion a year for the wealthfare portion of homeowners' tax breaks.

Now if you introduced legislation to provide $26 billion in housing subsidies to wealthy families, it wouldn't stand a chance (although we probably shouldn't put anything past

Congress). But because these provisions are called "deductions" and "exemptions" rather than "subsidies," they're enshrined in our current tax code, and middle-class homeowners think *they're* the ones getting the deal.

If you believe that, you're being had. It's a classic case of being tossed a few scraps from the table. If we simply eliminate all the hand-outs and boondoggles this book documents, our tax rates would drop so far, so fast, that special little deals like these homeowners' loopholes would seem archaic and silly.

AGRIBUSINESS SUBSIDIES

$18 BILLION A YEAR

When agricultural subsidies began during the Great Depression, their main purpose was to keep farmers on the farm, by enabling them to earn roughly what people in cities did. Today, the average full-time farmer is worth $700,000—almost nineteen times more than the average household—and farmers' per capita income from all sources has exceeded that of nonfarmers' income every year since 1986.

In 1994, the 16% of farms that had sales of $100,000 or more received 65% of all agricultural subsidies. In 1990, 90% of direct government payments went to the largest 18% of farms—mostly huge agribusiness conglomerates—while 64% of all farmers received nothing at all.

Not only is the US Department of Agriculture (USDA) quite generous in its handouts to farmers, it's also quite generous in who it calls a farmer. Over the last decade, it's doled out almost $2 billion to recipients in urban zip codes, and many recipients aren't even located in the same state as their farms. So if we put the word "farmers" in quotes below, you'll know why.

Agribusiness subsidies take several forms:

- With *price supports,* quasi-governmental agencies or cooperatives buy up "excess" production of a crop to keep the price high. (It's sort of like government-sanctioned price fixing.)

- *Production quotas* limit who can farm a particular crop (peanut and tobacco farmers, for example, must be licensed by the government).

- *Market quotas* control how much of a crop can be sold; the "excess" is warehoused or destroyed.

- *Import restrictions* limit how much of a crop can be imported into the US.

- Finally, there are *deficiency payments,* which we discuss on pp. 61–62.

The "cheaper food" ruse

One rationale for agribusiness subsidies—to the extent that they have any—is that you get cheaper food prices out of the deal. Dream on.

First of all, we pay for many of these handouts with our income taxes, so you'd have to add some portion of those taxes to your food bill to come up with an accurate total. Besides that, there are indirect subsidies you pay for at the checkout counter without even realizing it.

Price supports, import restrictions, and market and production quotas keep the prices of sugar, dairy products and peanuts higher in the US than they are on the world market. They cost consumers $1.4 billion a year in higher sugar prices, $2.5 billion in higher dairy prices and $500 million in higher peanut prices. That's $4.4 billion at the cash register right there.

Even when agribusiness subsidies actually do bring down the cost of food, you typically end up paying for them in other ways. For example, diverting productive salmon streams to grow crops in the desert may be great for fast-food outlets and for the corporate farmers who supply them, but it's hell on fishermen and recreational workers. Their unemployment insurance is part of the cost of your cheaper meal.

Livestock subsidies

Many Americans are cutting back on meat and dairy products for health reasons. But whatever your diet, you help pay for these products with your taxes (not to mention the Medicare costs of those who overconsume them).

While most farmers have to treat their profits as ordinary income, livestock profits are classified as capital gains and taxed at a lower rate (currently 28%). But the costs of buying, breeding and raising livestock are ordinary expenses that can be deducted immediately. This best-of-both-worlds tax treatment encourages people to get into the livestock business, and there are nontax inducements as well.

Cattle ranchers graze their herds on public lands leased to them at about a quarter of their market value. In 1994, the BLM (Bureau of Land Management) took in $29 million from grazing leases and spent more than three times as much—$105 million—managing the lands.

Cattle trample native plants and grasses, foul local streams and contribute to erosion. Add in those environmental factors and the true cost of grazing leases comes to about $200 million a year (according to two conservative think tanks, the Competitive Enterprise Institute and the Cato Institute).

Like most agribusiness handouts, cattle subsidies go disproportionately to the very rich— 75% of the grazing land leased by the BLM is controlled by fewer than 10% of the lessees.

Subsidies for drug peddlers

But at least beef and milk are edible. Tobacco, a drug that kills 48 Americans every hour, is also subsidized with a combination of price supports, import restrictions and production and marketing quotas.

Rep. Richard Durbin (D–Illinois), who introduced a proposal to end tobacco subsidies, estimates their cost at about $41 million in fiscal 1997. (In addition, they generate higher costs to consumers of an estimated $857 million.) In June 1996, the House of Representatives voted down Durbin's measure by a smoke-thin margin of 212 to 210.

Usually the tobacco lobby does better than a two-vote margin. Its thirteen PACs, among the most generous on Capitol Hill, handed out almost $10 million between 1986 and 1995. (When you kill off 419,000 of your customers every year, you need all the friends you can get.)

Although the tobacco lobby has made sure that some portion of the federal government supports tobacco farmers, public pressure has forced other parts of the government to discourage smoking. Seeing the writing on the wall, US tobacco manufacturers are making a big push for new customers overseas. US tobacco exports have risen 275% since 1985, when we started threatening foreign countries like Japan, Thailand, South Korea and Taiwan with trade sanctions unless they opened their markets to US cigarettes.

Taiwan has been trying to restrict smoking in public areas, and to ban cigarette advertising and vending machine sales. That should sound familiar, because the same efforts are being made in this country. But when *they* do it, we call it an unfair trade practice.

If this hypocritical coercion of ours is successful, the results will be as disastrous for Taiwan as they were for South Korea. One year after the US tobacco giants penetrated that market, the smoking rate for teenage boys had almost doubled (from 18% to 30%), while the rate for teenage girls had more than quintupled (from 1.6% to 8.7%).

Deficiency payments

Like price supports, quotas and import restrictions, *deficiency payments* keep the cost of certain crops artificially high. In former years, they made up the difference between a target price set by the USDA and the actual market price for that year (so if the target price was $15 a bushel and the market price $12, the USDA gave farmers $3 a bushel). This smoothed out the highs and lows of commodity prices, which fluctuate with the weather and other factors.

Between 1985 and 1994, deficiency payments cost us an average of $8.3 billion a year (the range was $4.1 to $14.3 billion). Here's how they break down:

Corn: 45%
Wheat: 24%
Cotton: 12%
Rice: 7%
Sorghum: 4%
Dairy: 3%
Barley: 2%
Wool and mohair: 2%
Oats: 0.2%

Although supporters of the 1996 farm bill claim it will eliminate deficiency payments by 2002, it actually phases them down to a level of *$4 billion*, which is almost exactly what they were in 1994. It also replaces the old system with a flat rate. In bad years, farmers will get only the predetermined payments and no more, but in good years, they'll get the same amount, even if they rake in far more than the market price of their crop. This is what happened in 1996, when there were exceptionally high market prices for many of the subsidized crops, and the same is projected for 1997.

Only "farmers" who got deficiency payments before 1996 are eligible for them under the 1996 bill, and how much they get is determined by what they got before. There's no work requirement and there's no means test; they don't have to be active farmers or managers. If the price of corn hits $1000 a bushel, they get the payments. If they sit on a beach and let the crops rot in the field, they get the payments.

The top 2% of deficiency payments recipients will get 22% of the total subsidy. Almost 400 of them are eligible to get more than $1 million apiece (all they have to do is apply for it). The 1996 bill also allows recipients to keep $1.7 billion in deficiency payments from previous years that, under previous law, they would have had to apply against future payments.

Because overseas demand for US crops is expected to be strong well into the future, prices for major crops are forecast to be high for several years. Thus, according to USDA projections, the old system of deficiency payments would have cost an average of only $1¾ billion a year between 1996 and 2002. Under the 1996 farm bill, however, they're projected to average $5.1 billion a year— almost three times as much.

The waters of Babylon

Subsidized irrigation water is another good example of how agribusiness handouts distort our economic life. Because the official purpose of this program is to help small farmers, no farm larger than 960 acres is supposed to receive subsidized water. It hasn't quite worked out that way.

The giant agribusiness companies waltz around the 960-acre limit by setting up networks of corporations and trusts to disguise their massive land holdings. (They're not fooling anybody, of course, but their political clout prevents the law from being enforced.)

Technically, water users are also supposed to help pay for constructing irrigation projects, but the government charges no interest, waits ten years before starting to collect, and then only asks for $2\frac{1}{2}\%$ of the principal each year. Between 1902 (when the program began) and 1986, these policies cost us an estimated $70 billion in lost interest payments.

Once the canals are built, the water is provided free of charge—or at very low cost—though it isn't free to produce. It's estimated that irrigation projects, public dams and the sale of water at below-market prices cost us more than $3 billion a year nationwide. Small farmers get very little of the benefit from this. In California, corporate "farmers" like Southern Pacific, Chevron, Getty Oil, Shell Oil and Prudential Insurance use more than two-thirds of the state's agricultural water.

The main effect of irrigation subsidies is to encourage agribusiness to waste water, depleting the nation's watersheds as well as its treasury. Many subsidized irrigators actually turn around and sell their excess water at a profit—sometimes to local governments!

(Isn't free enterprise great? We spend a fortune on dams and canals so some bloated welfare parasite can sell water *we paid for* back to us *at a profit*. We pay for it once with our federal taxes and then we pay for it *again*—at a higher price—with our local taxes.)

Miscellaneous pork

- The Conservation Reserve Program paid farmers $1.8 billion in fiscal 1996 (including administrative costs) not to grow crops on their land. Supposedly this is to help control soil erosion, but much of the erosion is caused by unsustainable farming practices.

- The USDA funds various research programs that help farmers take advantage of new technologies, improve the quality of agricultural products and find new uses for them. One program even funds marketing research for farmers. Agribusiness derives the benefits from all this, but it doesn't pay the $1.7 billion a year it costs. We do.

- The National Agricultural Statistics Service collects and publishes data on agricultural crops and farm program payments, at a cost of $81 million a year.

The welfare king

No discussion of agribusiness would be complete without the story of Dwayne Andreas, the undisputed king of American welfare. The Cato

Institute estimates that his company, Archer Daniels Midland (ADM), derives at least 43% of its profits from products that are heavily subsidized or protected by the US government.

But Andreas knows how to share. Back in 1972, he stopped by the Nixon White House to personally hand over an envelope that contained $100,000 in hundred-dollar bills. Later on, he sent a check for $25,000 that was cashed by Watergate burglar Bernard Barker.

Not only are Andreas and his family among the top contributors to Bill Clinton, he's also #4 on Bob Dole's list of top career contributors—and that doesn't include the $100,000 he gave to Bob Dole's Better America foundation, or the apartment the Doles bought from an Andreas-controlled company at well below market value, or the dozens of free trips Dole has taken on ADM corporate jets, or the million dollars Andreas' ADM foundation gave to the Red Cross after Dole's wife Liddy became its president.

In 1992, Andreas gave a combined total of $1.4 million to the Republican and Democratic parties. According to the *Wall Street Journal*, his political contributions between 1979 and 1995 came to more than $4 million.

Andreas calls this "tithing." And what does he get in return for it? Plenty. ADM has profited from deficiency payments on corn, sugar quotas and subsidized grain exports. Then there's the tax credit for ethanol production.

The ethanol handout

There are lots of kinds of alcohol. *Ethanol* is the scientific name for the kind that's in alcoholic beverages. When one part ethanol is added to nine parts gasoline, the result is *gasohol.* Like the ethanol in bourbon, the ethanol that's added to gasoline is made from corn (something ADM grows a *lot* of).

Gasohol is a cleaner-burning fuel, but since ethanol only contains about two-thirds as much energy as gasoline, gasohol doesn't work as well as gasoline. The DOE (US Department of Energy) calculates that gasohol-powered vehicles average 4.7 fewer miles per gallon than gasoline-powered vehicles.

Not only that, but ethanol costs nearly twice as much to produce as gas. And the process is much less efficient. According to ADM's own figures, so much natural gas and electricity is required that the net energy gain is only about 12%.

But even that measly 12% gain is vastly overstated. It doesn't take into account the fact that many ethanol producers burn coal, which is less efficient than natural gas, nor does it include the energy spent growing the corn, powering the tractors that harvest it, or fueling the trucks that haul it to the production facility.

Factor all that in and you get an amazing picture. According to the DOE, producing a gallon of ethanol results in a net energy *loss* of between 11% and 16%!

How can anyone make money on that? Welcome to the ethanol tax credit. Companies receive a tax break of 5.4¢ for each gallon of gasohol sold; since one gallon of ethanol makes ten gallons of gasohol (there's no tax break for the gasoline portion), this translates to 54¢ for each gallon of ethanol used.

In 1994, when a barrel of oil cost $18, this tax break was equivalent to a subsidy of $23 for each barrel of ethanol produced. In other words, for $5 less than we're paying merely to subsidize gasohol production, we could buy a barrel of oil flat out!

You can see why there'd be no market for ethanol without the subsidy, which cost us $625 million in 1995. ADM made 60% of all the ethanol produced in the United States that year, which means that taxpaying schnooks like us contributed about $375 million to subsidize Dwayne Andreas' bottom line. (No other federal subsidy went so disproportionately to one company that year.)

How sweet it is

ADM does a triple-dip into our pockets. First they profit from the price supports on corn. Then they turn a bunch of the corn into sweetener, the price of which is kept artificially high by import restrictions and market quotas on sugar. (If sugar were cheaper, corn sweetener would have to be cheaper too, in order to compete.) Finally, some of the corn is turned into subsidized ethanol.

Call us crazy, but we think all this may have something to do with Andreas' "tithing."

Maybe it's just a coincidence, but just days after Andreas contributed $100,000 to a presidential dinner, President Clinton issued an order that 30% of the gasoline in nine US cities must contain ethanol.

As for Bob Dole, he's been as devoted to Andreas as an old hunting dog. He kept the 54¢ a gallon credit from being applied to competing gasoline additives like methanol (wood alcohol)—which is too bad, since methanol is cheaper, easier to get to market and burns cleaner. Dole also helped impose tariffs on imported alcohol fuels.

Walk in. Pig out.

There used to be a ribs place in Berkeley that had that motto painted on its window (maybe it still does). It would serve as a wonderful slogan for the USDA as well.

Let's review what's in the agribusiness trough. Price supports, import restrictions, and production and marketing quotas on sugar, peanuts and dairy products cost us $4.4 billion a year; on tobacco, they cost almost $900 million. We lose about $200 million a year on grazing leases.

Under the 1996 farm bill, deficiency payments should average about $5.1 billion a year. Subsidized irrigation water costs more than $3 billion. We lose about $3.6 billion to the programs listed under *Miscellaneous pork*, and $625 million to the ethanol subsidy.

The total agribusiness pig-out amounts to almost $18 billion per year. And that doesn't include export subsidies (see that chapter for details) or the damage to our health and to the environment—both here and abroad—that's caused by current USDA policies.

TAX AVOIDANCE BY TRANSNATIONALS

$12 BILLION A YEAR

"Why, man, he doth bestride the narrow world like a colossus, and we petty men walk under his huge legs, and peep about to find ourselves dishonorable graves." Cassius' description of Caesar is hard to beat for giving the flavor of how transnational corporations have come to dominate the earth. (A *transnational*—or *multinational*—corporation is simply one that has operations in more than one country.)

Richer than many nations, more powerful than most, transnationals lumber about, settling where taxes are lowest and labor is cheapest and most intimidated. But many are still headquartered in the US, and virtually all of them have significant operations here. That brings up the sticky question of US taxes.

Not to worry. Both US- and foreign-based transnationals have lots of tricks for avoiding our taxes.

The transfer pricing shell game
For the most part, the IRS simply takes a transnational's word for how much taxable income it earns in this country. Conducting

an audit requires the IRS to look at every transaction between the domestic and foreign branches of the corporation, and then assess whether a fair price was charged for that transaction.

Because that's an impossible task, corporations feel free to shift profits out of, and expenses into, the US—thus minimizing, on paper, the profitability of their US-based operations. This is called *transfer pricing.*

There's an easy way to cut through the trickery of transfer pricing. Called the *unitary method,* it calculates taxes based simply on how much of the company's sales, assets and payroll are in the US (or any other country).

The unitary method is more accurate and easier to enforce, and makes it far more difficult for companies to hide their profits in offshore tax shelters. That's why it's so fiercely opposed by transnational corporations and their congressional hirelings.

Of the US-based transnationals with assets over $100 million, 37% paid no US federal taxes at all in 1991, and the average tax rate for those that did pay was just 1% of gross receipts! (We'd tell you what it was as a percentage of profits, but nobody knows. That's just the point—they avoid paying tax by concealing how much profit they make.)

Foreign-based transnationals did even better. 71% of them paid no US income tax on their operations in this country, and the average rate for those that did pay was just 0.6%—*six-tenths of one percent*—of gross receipts! (You can see why they'd be anxious to avoid a tax burden like *that.)*

How successful foreign-based transnationals are at avoiding taxes has a lot to do with where they're based. In 1989, only 22% of Swedish-based transnationals managed the trick, compared to 64% of the British-based, 73% of the Japanese, 78% of the Dutch, 92% of the Panamanian and 95% of the Irish. The Saudis took the cake—99% of the transnational corporations based in Saudi Arabia paid no US income tax on the profits they earned in the US.

The Puerto Rican exemption

In 1976, Congress decided to boost employment in Puerto Rico by completely exempting companies from taxes on the profits they made there. Between then and 1994, companies from the US mainland earned $35 billion in profits in Puerto Rico and paid not a penny of federal tax on that.

The pharmaceutical industry has made particular use of this tax break by writing off the cost of developing drugs—much of which is taxpayer-subsidized—on their US tax returns, then producing the drugs in Puerto Rico, so they can assign the profits to their subsidiaries there and pay no taxes on them. (Puerto Rico also offers exemptions from income, property, municipal and excise taxes.)

President Reagan tried to eliminate the Puerto Rican tax exemption in 1986, but failed in the face of fierce industry lobbying. In 1993, President Clinton succeeded in scaling it back somewhat, so US companies in Puerto Rico will only escape some $30 billion in taxes during the 1990s, rather than the $40 billion they would have avoided if the law hadn't been changed.

Credit for foreign taxes

US-based transnationals are also allowed to credit any taxes paid to foreign governments against taxes they owe here. Supposedly this is to prevent companies from being taxed twice on the same income. The problem is, there's no efficient way to make sure that a company is telling a foreign country the same thing it tells us.

There are rules to prevent this sort of abuse, of course, but companies can still find plenty of ways around them. In the late 1940s, when the king of Saudi Arabia began demanding higher royalty rates of American oil companies operating there, they suggested that he simply impose a corporate income tax on them instead. They'd pay no more in total taxes, but the king would get higher payments. Soon the other countries in the Persian Gulf all had corporate income taxes as well.

Sometimes lying isn't necessary. After making millions of dollars from selling computer chips in Japan, Intel was able to exempt the profits from US tax by convincing US Tax Court that they were Japanese income. But a tax treaty between the two countries requires Japan to treat the profits as American income, therefore exempting them from Japanese tax! Thus the profits became "nowhere income"—

not taxable anywhere. This happens more often than you might think.

There's one further problem with this set-up. By treating US state and local taxes as deductions against federal income tax, while treating foreign taxes as a credit (which is much more valuable), our tax code creates an incentive to ship US jobs abroad.

What it costs

While every expert source considers tax avoidance by transnational corporations to be a major problem, they disagree on the extent of it. So we'll just pick one knowledgeable source. According to Citizens for Tax Justice, reducing tax avoidance by transnational corporations would save us $12.2 billion in 1997 (let's round that off to $12 billion) and $15.6 billion in the year 2002.

TAX-FREE MUNI BONDS

$9.1 BILLION A YEAR

To help attract investors to bonds issued by state and local governments—generally called *municipal bonds, muni bonds* or simply *munis*—the federal government has made the interest on most of them exempt from federal income tax.

Leaving aside the question of how worthy the projects are that munis finance—they can be anything from water treatment plants to prisons—these tax exemptions cost the US

Treasury a lot more than they save state and local governments.

According to Citizens for Tax Justice (CTJ), interest rates on long-term munis averaged around 5.8% in the mid-1990s, while rates on comparable taxable Treasury and corporate bonds averaged 7.6% (after subtracting any state taxes that were due). This means state and local governments were able to pay 24% less interest to investors than they would have had to pay if the interest on their bonds were taxable.

But most of that interest went to wealthy investors in tax brackets substantially higher than 24%. So while state and local governments are saving 24% on the bonds, corporations are saving between 34% and 39% and wealthy individuals between 31% and almost 40%.

The difference between those rates and 24% represents the net loss to government on all levels. (What's more, if the muni bond is from the same state as the taxpayer, the interest on it is exempt from state income tax as well.)

CTJ estimates that, overall, only 46% of this muni-bond subsidy actually benefits state and local governments, while 27% goes to individual investors, 18% to corporations and 9% to nonprofit hospitals and schools. In the end, "about a quarter of the federal subsidy ends up as a windfall to well-off investors." Since the total tax subsidy is expected to cost the federal government $36.4 billion a year between 1996 and 2002, the wealthfare portion of it runs $9.1 billion a year (a quarter of $36.4 billion).

But that's not the worst of it. To quote CTJ again: "In many circumstances, private companies and individuals can 'borrow' the ability to issue tax-free bonds from state and local governments."

Before the mid-1980s, "there was almost no limit on what states could authorize tax-exempt financing for—and since the federal government was picking up the bill, there was no [reason for] the states [not to go] hog-wild. Reforms now generally limit the total amount...but it still remains a major drain on the federal Treasury." In fact, CTJ estimates that about 36% of all muni-bond revenues finance private projects.

MEDIA HANDOUTS

$8 BILLION A YEAR

Officially, the Communications Act of 1934 declared that "the airwaves belong to the people." What it actually did was hand out portions of the airwaves free to businesses, which then made as much money off them as they could, without having to pay the government anything for the privilege.

Thanks—at least in part—to this generosity, the combined profits of the four largest television networks were $2½ billion in 1994 (on revenues of almost $15 billion). One of the TV channels the government gave away in New York was recently purchased by Dow Jones and ITT for $207 million.

Broadcasters have been paying less and less lip service to the toothless "public service" requirements of their licenses. That's understandable, since none of them has ever had a serious challenge from the FCC (the Federal Communications Commission)—not even General Electric, which owns NBC and has been convicted of many felonies (for details on some of them, see the section on career criminals in the chapter on military waste and fraud).

Give them a finger and they want a hand

The government and the electronics industry want to encourage the development of high-definition television (HDTV). While we're shifting to that new standard, TV stations will need to broadcast two signals—one for the TV sets we all have now, and one for new sets that receive HDTV.

To make that transition as painless as possible, the FCC proposes giving TV broadcasters an extra, free channel for each one they currently control—both for VHF (channels 2 through 13) and UHF (channels 14 through 69). Eventually, the FCC wants to narrow TV's *spectrum* (portion of the airwaves), so that it only runs from channel 7 to channel 51. Needless to say, the broadcasters applaud the first part of the proposal and oppose the second.

Ironically, new digital technology makes it possible to broadcast up to six channels in the same amount of spectrum currently used for one—which means the broadcasters don't actually *need* the new, free spectrum in order to transition to HDTV. That hasn't stopped them from running zillions of commercials warning us that free television will disappear if they don't get this handout. (They urge you to write your representatives in Congress. So do we.)

Broadcasters are used to getting spectrum for free, but since 1992, new *spectra* (that's the plural) have been auctioned off. For example, cellular phone companies paid $10 billion for theirs in 1994, and eighteen mobile phone and pager licenses went for $904 million at a 1996 auction.

The FCC estimates that the TV channels they want to give away would fetch $37 billion if auctioned off. Since there are the same number of these proposed new channels as the ones the broadcasters currently control, we can assume the latter are also worth $37 billion.

So if we forced TV broadcasters to pay for what they've been using for free for more than six decades, we'd have an extra $37 billion in the Treasury. That means the government could issue $37 billion less in Treasury bonds. Assuming they'd pay about 7% on the bonds, having the $37 billion in hand would lower the deficit by $2.6 billion each year (7% of $37 billion).

The radio spectra

AM and FM radio slots were also given to broadcasters free of charge. When they sell them to *each other,* however, they don't continue that tradition. A radio station in a major market can run as high as $100 million, and it's rare for a station to be sold for less than $100,000, even in the smallest town. Here are some recent valuations:

According to *US News and World Report,* the 21 radio stations Disney acquired when it bought ABC were worth $2 billion—more than $95 million each. After Westinghouse bought CBS, the 39 radio stations it controlled were worth $1 billion—almost $26 million each.

Twelve stations in Texas recently sold for $306.5 million (almost $26 million each) and nineteen more there went for $395 million (about $21 million each). Two stations in Norfolk, Virginia cost $8.1 million, and another one there $6.5 million. Five suburban stations—three in Patterson, New York and two in Danbury, Connecticut—brought in $15 million ($3 million each).

In that random sample, the average price is almost $38 million per radio station. (Some of that goes for electronic equipment and the like, but the license—the right to broadcast on a particular band of the radio spectrum—makes up most of the value.)

Let's be ultraconservative and say that the average radio station license is worth a million dollars. There are approximately 14,000 stations in the US. So, if we forced radio broadcasters to pay for what they've been using for free, we'd have *at least* an extra $14 billion in the Treasury. Not having to issue

7% bonds for that amount would save us $980 million a year. (Since this is such a loose estimate, and almost certainly way too low, let's just call it an even billion.)

Reducing the advertising deduction

The unlimited deductibility of advertising as a business expense is an indirect subsidy to the media (print as well as broadcast). Why, you ask, is that a form of wealthfare? Well, for one thing, it's only available to businesses; ordinary taxpayers can't deduct the cost of running an ad in the paper to sell their car, or to find a babysitter for the kids.

Second, like any deduction, it's worth more to corporations and other higher-bracket taxpayers than it is to the average person. Third, it subsidizes ads we also regulate—such as those for liquor or cigarettes, or ones aimed at children—which means we're paying these companies with our right hand to do something we're trying to get them to stop doing with our left hand.

Finally, it allows the broadcast media to sell something—access to the airwaves—that we gave them for free. (Sure, their programming has increased the value of those airwaves, but that can't be the whole story, since—as we've seen—buying a station costs *a lot* of money, and the programming doesn't come with it.)

In 1994, corporate America spent $150 billion on advertising (in all media). One proposal calls for scaling back the deductibility of advertising from 100% to 80%, as was done with business meals and entertainment in 1986 (they're now down to 50%), and allowing the remaining 20% to be amortized over four years. That modest plan would reduce the federal deficit by about $4.4 billion a year.

To that let's add the $2.6 billion a year it costs us not to auction off the existing TV spectra away, and the $1 billion it costs us for the free radio spectra. This gives us a total for media handouts of $8 billion a year.

EXCESSIVE GOVERNMENT PENSIONS

$7.6 BILLION A YEAR

Most federal employees enjoy a number of benefits not found in the private sector. The main perk is the ability to retire with full benefits after 30 years of service—or just 20 in the military. As a result, the average age of federal retirees is 58, compared to 63 in the private sector. (The average military retiree spends 22 years earning a pension and 35 years collecting it!)

All federal pensions have automatic cost-of-living adjustments (COLAs) set at 100% of the consumer price index (CPI). Thanks to these, many civil service retirees get bigger checks than the people who are now doing their jobs! Only 5% of private pension plans have automatic COLAs, and very few of those increase by 100% of the CPI. (About half of state and local pensions have automatic COLAs.)

In 1992, when the average private pension was around $600 a month, the average government pension was $1420 a month—more than twice as much. It used to be that government workers received bigger pensions because they were paid less, but during the last 40 years, federal salaries have risen 25% faster than those in the private sector.

In 1991, $9.2 billion in pension payments went to households whose annual incomes (including salaries from jobs they took after retirement, investment income, retirement benefits, etc.) were over $100,000. Former Speaker of the House Tom Foley's pension started at $123,804 a year—COLAs will increase that every year—and Dan Rostenkowski's at $96,468 (formerly chairman of the powerful House Ways and Means Committee, he can even collect that money in prison—which is fortunate, since that's where he now resides).

In 1994, government pensions cost us $65 billion. About 58% of that—$38 billion—is beyond what private companies would pay, on average, to people with the same salary histories. If public employees' pensions were equivalent to those in the private sector, the average person's income tax would drop by 8%.

Although most—if not all—of that $38 billion is excessive, a lot of it benefits people who aren't rich. To come up with a figure for the wealthfare portion of it, we've used the fact that we'd save $7.6 billion a year just by shaving 25% off government pensions paid to households with annual incomes of $70,000 or more. That's a pretty conservative estimate of how much welfare for the rich there is in excessive government pensions.

(Like the Social Security trust fund, the government pension fund hasn't been managed very carefully, and already owes $870 billion more than is in it; if you include state and military pensions, the figure is $1.7 *trillion*. All that money will either have to be borrowed, raised through taxes, or cut out of some other part of the budget.)

INSURANCE LOOPHOLES

$7.2 BILLION A YEAR

If you heard that Wal-Mart, America's biggest retailer, spends around $1 billion a year on life insurance it gives free of charge to about 325,000 of its employees, your initial reaction would probably be, "Isn't that nice? Some big companies really *do* care about their workers." Unfortunately, there's a twist to the story.

Eeek!—COLI
To encourage workers to sign up for the insurance, Wal-Mart offers them other free benefits. They'll even continue to pay for the policy after you leave their employ.

Now you're probably feeling a little confused. Why should Wal-Mart offer additional inducements to get employees to sign up for free insurance? And why in the world would they continue coverage for people who no longer work for them?

The answer's very simple. When an employee dies, *Wal-Mart*—not the employee's heirs—collects $60,000! Out of that, they give the heirs $5000—about 8%. (If the insured was a former employee, the heirs get just $1000; if the death was accidental, they get $10,000.)

This boondoggle is called *corporate-owned life insurance,* or *COLI.* It's designed to avoid taxes by taking advantage of the fact that life insurance proceeds are tax-free. In 1994, Wal-Mart used COLI to save $36 million in taxes; in 1995, they saved an estimated $80 million.

"But wait," you say, "the insurance costs them $1 billion a year, right?" Wrong. It costs them nothing.

They borrow money to pay the premiums from the same company that sells them the insurance (in effect, the insurance company bills the premiums, pays them itself, and charges Wal-Mart interest). When an employee (or former employee) dies, Wal-Mart uses the insurance proceeds—minus the pittance they send to the heirs—to pay off the loans they got from the insurance company.

But what about the interest Wal-Mart has to pay on those loans from the insurance company? Well, first of all, like all business interest, it's tax-deductible. Secondly, they don't actually *pay* the interest—they borrow *more* money to cover it, and the interest on *those* loans is also tax-deductible. So, in a nutshell, COLI allows companies to deduct from their taxes all the interest on these loans, then lets them pay back the loans themselves with tax-free insurance proceeds.

Originally promoted as a tax break for small businesses, COLI has ended up benefiting giant corporations like Disney, Coca-Cola and AT&T, at a cost to the US Treasury of about $1.5 billion a year. It's survived a move in Congress to abolish it, thanks to strong lobbying from the insurance industry.

Other loopholes

COLI is far from the only loophole available in the creative world of insurance. Companies whose net income from premiums is less than $350,000 a year are tax-exempt. Those whose net premium income falls between $350,000 and $2.1 million get to pay tax on either their investment income or their premium income, whichever is less; the other income is tax-free.

Life insurance companies get to deduct the entire amount they set aside as a reserve each year, whether or not it exceeds the actual amount they have to pay out in claims. (Needless to say, this gives them a powerful incentive to increase the size of the reserve.) Property and casualty companies get a similar deduction. Between them, these reserve loopholes cost us more than $4 billion a year.

If you run a certain type of nonprofit organization—a fraternal society, say, or a voluntary employee benefit association—you might want to consider setting up your own in-house insurance operation. It won't be taxed either, and you can pay huge salaries to your top executives, just like any other self-respecting insurance company.

The insurance industry has carved out several other loopholes for itself. Put them all together and they cost you about $7.2 billion a year.

NUCLEAR SUBSIDIES

$7.1 BILLION A YEAR

As Noam Chomsky points out, most successful US industries wouldn't be competitive internationally if the federal government hadn't developed their basic technology with your tax dollars, then given it away to private companies. Computers, biotech and commercial aviation are examples, and so—preeminently—is nuclear power. Nuclear power still can't stand on its own two feet, but with a sugar daddy like the federal government, it doesn't need to.

The feds still provide the industry with most of its fuel and waste disposal, and much of its research. Between 1948 and 1995, the government spent more than $61 billion (in 1995 dollars) on nuclear power research—almost two-thirds of all federal support for energy research and development. The 1996 figure was $468 million.

The insurance subsidy

Since 1959, the government has also limited the liability of nuclear utilities for damage caused by accidents. Until 1988, the utilities were only responsible for the first $560 million per accident; then the limit was raised to $7 billion.

But $7 billion wouldn't begin to cover the costs of a core meltdown, or even a near-meltdown like Chernobyl. That accident's total costs are estimated at $358 billion—not to mention the 125,000 deaths the Ukrainian government figures it has caused.

The Energy Information Administration calculates that if nuclear utilities were required to buy insurance coverage above that $7 billion on the open market, it would cost almost $28 million per reactor, for a total annual subsidy of $3 billion. (Even if it could pay its own way, the risks of nuclear power far outweigh its benefits. But that's the subject for another book.)

Enriched uranium fuel

Before 1993, the DOE (Department of Energy) was responsible for all domestic production of enriched uranium fuel for nuclear power plants. Since then, that's been the job of a government corporation called the US Enrichment Corporation (USEC). The USEC has been a financial disaster, even for a government program; taking into account lingering liabilities like environmental cleanups, it's more than $10 billion in the hole.

Having made a fine mess of things, the government plans to privatize the USEC. Naturally, they'll try to give the private company buying USEC as many assets as possible, and keep as many liabilities as they can, so that we and our children can pay for them. For example, the DOE plans to take large amounts of radioactive waste from the eventually privatized corporation, even though it has no place to safely store them. These liabilities will cost taxpayers an estimated $1.1 billion.

But wait—there's more. We lose on the selling price too, which the GAO (Government Accounting Office) estimates at $1.7 to $2.2 billion. Since the net present value of USEC cash flows is $2.8 to $3.5 billion, taxpayers would be out between $600 million and $1.8 billion on the deal. So the total we'll pay for privatizing the USEC will fall between $1.7 and $2.9 billion.

Reprocessing fuel rods

Nuclear power plants create radioactive waste. Naturally, the government feels that it's our responsibility as taxpayers to take this waste and either reprocess it into new fuel rods or find some place to store it for the next 10,000 years or so. Let's talk about reprocessing first.

Argonne National Laboratory (outside of Chicago) used to operate an enormously expensive facility for separating plutonium, uranium and the like from spent nuclear fuel rods, so that these elements could be used in new fuel rods or nuclear weapons. In 1994, Congress killed funding for that, but the same sort of reprocessing is still taking place in Idaho, at an annual cost to us of $25 million. And Argonne is still getting $25 million a year to terminate its program.

The Savannah River site in South Carolina was originally used for weapons production. As a result of that activity, several square miles of land are so badly contaminated that human beings will probably never be able to use them again. This site is now used for reprocessing spent and corroded fuel rods, and may reprocess foreign fuel rods as well. This new business is going to cost us $340 million a year.

Their waste—our responsibility

A place like Savannah River naturally brings the subject of waste to mind. Nobody wants nuclear waste stored in their state, so Congress picked a place in Nevada, a state with little congressional clout. Called Yucca Mountain, it's the least stable site of any considered to date, with 33 known earthquake faults in the area.

Work on Yucca Mountain can't proceed until the Supreme Court rules on a law Nevada passed that prohibits the storage of nuclear waste in the state. Yucca Mountain's planned opening has been moved back from 1998 to 2015, but we're still being charged $250 million a year just to study the situation.

If Yucca Mountain does go ahead, it will cost us $33 billion—some say $40 or $50 billion—to build the facility, transport radioactive waste to it from all over the country, and seal the waste into thousands of containers. Meanwhile, there are *no* long-term storage sites for nuclear waste (and Yucca may never be one either).

The nuclear industry is lobbying hard to build a vastly inadequate short-term storage facility above ground at Yucca Mountain. Their eagerness is explained by the fact that once they turn the waste over to Uncle Sam, it's our problem, not theirs. The Public Interest Research Group (PIRG) says that this whole boondoggle has the potential to turn into "the S&L bailout of the Nineties."

Yucca Mountain is supposed to be financed by the Nuclear Waste Fund, which is generated by charging utility customers a fee of $\frac{1}{10}$¢ per kilowatt hour for nuclear-generated power. But in its thirteen years of existence, the fund has never been adjusted for inflation, which has cut its purchasing power by 45%.

There's another catch: The funds come from existing reactors, and no new ones are on order in the US. As the old reactors are retired, the fund's revenues will decline and ultimately disappear, leaving taxpayers holding the bag.

And there's *another* problem: Money in the fund is currently being used to pay for interim storage, which depletes the amount available for Yucca Mountain (or whatever long-term storage site is eventually decided on). If everything remains unchanged, the Nuclear Waste Fund will fall $4–$8 billion (in 1995 dollars) short of the money it needs, according to the DOE and the State of Nevada.

The cost of closing them down

Nuclear reactors are licensed to operate for 40 years, but only one has survived past 30.

Of the 110 reactors in the US, only three have begun to be "decommissioned" (closed down), but 25 others will need to be soon.

The Yankee Rowe plant in Massachusetts, the nation's first commercial reactor, was the first to begin the process (except for the Shoreham plant on Long Island, which only operated for 300 hours). How much will decommissioning Yankee Rowe cost? The figure continues to rise; the owner's latest guess is $375 million— ten times what it cost to build the plant. Other estimates go as high as $500 million.

Let's say it costs about $400 million, on average, to decommission a nuclear reactor. That means that closing down 25 plants will cost about $10 billion, which is more than the nuclear industry has set aside for all 107 remaining plants. Decommissioning *all* the plants will cost almost $42 billion.

The utilities are supposed to maintain a trust fund for decommissioning each plant. Chicago's Commonwealth Edison owns six elderly nukes, which will cost close to $2 billion to decommission; it has about $542 million set aside in trust funds for this purpose. Assuming this 73% shortfall is typical of the industry, the public's eventual share of the cost of closing all nuclear power plants will run more than $30 billion.

To help bail the industry out, Congress dropped the corporate tax rate on the industry's decommissioning trust funds from 34% to 20%. This has cost taxpayers $76 million for the five years from 1992 through 1996, and it's projected to rise to "several hundred million more" in the future. The nuclear industry is lobbying for relaxed restrictions on what they can put the trust funds' money into, obviously hoping that riskier investments will make up some of the shortfall.

A sympathetic federal appeals court has ruled that instead of decommissioning them, the utilities could turn their nuclear power plants into "sealed waste sites" for some unspecified period of time. This will probably make the eventual decommissioning even more expensive, since these reactors weren't designed to be used as storage facilities.

There's another problem with that plan. Because nuclear power plants need some place to discharge the water that cools the reactor, they're all situated near large bodies of water—usually rivers. Rivers flood at least every hundred years, which is a fraction of a second compared to the half-life of radioactive waste. Lakes can flood too, given enough rainfall. And if ocean levels rise significantly over the next century—as is predicted—seaside plants would also be threatened by high tides.

One way or another, the decommissioning of all these reactors will have to be paid for. It's not likely the utilities will cover the costs themselves. They'll probably leave the government to pick up the tab, along the lines of the S&L bailout.

Fusion research

Compared to fission (the process used by all commercial nuclear reactors to date), fusion—

the way the sun makes power—is much cleaner, safer and cheaper. *Theoretically*, that is. A few practical design problems crop up when you try to build a fusion reactor smaller than the sun.

Fusion research has been going on for more than 40 years, but even its most optimistic proponents admit that commercial applications can't be expected until the middle of the next century. While commercially viable reactors would theoretically—there's that word again—generate no waste, the currently existing experimental ones use radioactive tritium as a fuel and generate large amounts of waste.

A 1991 DOE memo that evaluated energy options in terms of economics and environmental risk ranked fusion 22nd out of 23. Despite that, the DOE spent $244 million on fusion research in fiscal 1996.

(Here's a little insight into how Congress works. The House originally approved $229 million and the Senate $225 million. When they got together to work out a compromise, they came up with $244 million!)

The "next generation" of nuclear plants

There hasn't been a nuclear power plant built in this country since 1973, and 89% of all utilities say they would never order one. So, naturally, our government is busy funding development of "the next generation of nuclear plants." For fiscal 1996, the DOE contributed $40 million to a consortium of companies—including GE (which recently became the world's largest company) and Westinghouse. The DOE even helps consortium members deal with the Nuclear Regulatory Commission's approval process for new technology.

Since there's no market for nuclear reactors in the US, any new reactors built here will probably be sold to East Asian countries. In fact, reactors based on the consortium's designs are already being built in Japan and have been offered to Taiwan—which shows that they're commercially viable and don't need continuing government support.

Adding it all up

- The government spent $468 million on nuclear research in 1996.

- The nuclear industry's insurance subsidy runs $3 billion a year.

- Privatizing uranium fuel enrichment will end up costing us between $1.7 and $2.9 billion. Let's take an average ($2.3 billion) and say the government issues 7% bonds to pay for it. The interest on those bonds will cost us $161 million a year.

- Reprocessing spent fuel rods costs us $390 million a year ($340 million in South Carolina, $25 million in Illinois, $25 million in Idaho).

- Just planning for long-term storage of nuclear waste currently costs us $250 million a year.

- Estimates of the shortfall in the Nuclear Waste Fund range from $4 billion to $8 billion, and will go on virtually forever. Let's take an average ($6 billion) and issue 7% bonds; interest on them will run $420 million a year.

- Closing nuclear power plants is already costing us $15 million a year in lost taxes (a figure that's projected to rise substantially).

- But the real cost will come when the utilities admit they haven't set enough money aside to do the job. If we have to pay for the estimated $30+ billion shortfall with 7% bonds, the yearly interest will run about $2.1 billion.

- Fusion research cost us $244 million in fiscal 1996.

- Development of the "next generation" of nuclear plants cost us $40 million in fiscal 1996.

Put all these numbers together and you get a total subsidy for nuclear power of almost $7.1 billion a year.

AVIATION SUBSIDIES

$5.5 BILLION A YEAR

The Seattle aerospace giant Boeing is being pinched by competition from Airbus, a European manufacturer that's supported, to the tune of about $300 million a year, by the governments of Germany, France, Britain and Spain. Boeing argues that these subsidies amount to an unfair trade practice— conveniently forgetting that US aerospace firms get about $1 billion a year in military research and development assistance from our government.

If there's an argument for governmental subsidies, it's that they help "infant industries" get on their feet. Commercial aviation is hardly an infant industry anymore, yet the government still pays for the air traffic control system, hands out grants for airport construction and provides reports from the National Weather Service. The Commerce Department lobbies aggressively for foreign purchases of US-built aircraft, and the airlines are exempted from the 4.3¢ per gallon fuel tax.

The Congressional Black Caucus says we can save $1.7 billion a year by cutting FAA airport grants, and raise $357 million a year by charging fees for landing rights at just four airports (O'Hare, JFK, La Guardia and DC National). They also advocate eliminating the Essential Air Service program, which subsidizes 82 small airports around the country, mostly in wealthy communities.

Overall, the aviation industry gets an estimated $4.5 billion a year in governmental subsidies—and that's above and beyond the $1 billion it receives in military research funds.

BUSINESS MEALS AND ENTERTAINMENT

$5.5 BILLION A YEAR

When the 1986 tax reform lowered the deductibility of business meals and entertainment from 100% to 80%, the restaurant industry worried that businesspeople would stop eating out—or that, at the very least, they'd shift from expensive restaurants to fast-food outlets. Neither of those things happened, nor were there any appreciable job

losses when the deduction was lowered further, to 50%, in 1993.

But even if there had been, that still
wouldn't justify continuing this loophole.
Money not spent on entertainment is likely to
be spent on other business expenses, and will
create other jobs to compensate for those lost
waiting tables. Or, if it isn't spent, corporate
overhead will go down and—ultimately—so
will the price of products and services.

The meals and entertainment deduction
amounts to an annual subsidy of $5.5 billion
for fancy restaurants, golf courses, skyboxes
at sports arenas and the like. And it's applied
unequally. Factory workers can't deduct
meals or sporting events at which they discuss their jobs with colleagues—nor can any
taxpayer who doesn't itemize deductions.

Like any deduction, this one is worth more
to higher-bracket taxpayers, and it's particularly subject to fraud and abuse. Since the
chance of an audit is low, the odds favor taxpayers who take an aggressive stance on the
deductibility of their entertainment expenses.

MINING SUBSIDIES

$3.5 BILLION A YEAR

Interior Secretary Bruce Babbitt was visibly
angry. He was about to sign away federal
land containing $68 million in gold for a total
price of $540, but he had no choice. The best

he could do was hold a news conference that featured a giant gift-wrapped box, and call the deal "a massive rip-off of the taxpayers."

Babbitt's hands were tied by a law that had been passed 123 years earlier, in the ultracorrupt administration of Ulysses S. Grant. Called the Mining Law of 1872, it was originally designed to encourage settlement of the West.

The Law of '72 allows anyone—including foreign corporations—to search for minerals on public lands and, when they find them, to "patent" the mineral rights *at the 1872 price*—which is never more than $5 an acre! *(Patenting* means the company gets to use the land as long as it's mining it.) More than 3.2 million acres—an area almost the size of Connecticut—have been given away at these ridiculous prices.

A Canadian mining company called American Barrick is in the process of extracting more than $10 billion in gold—$8¾ billion so far—from land in Nevada it paid $5,190 for. The Chevron and Manville corporations hope to lay their hands on about $4 billion worth of platinum and palladium; to patent the Montana acre where the minerals are found, they'll pay about $10,000.

Royalties? We don't pay no stinkin' royalties.
Since 1872, about $245 billion worth of minerals have been mined from public lands. And how much has our government collected in royalties? Absolutely nothing. Royalties aren't mentioned in the Law of '72, nor in any mining law since.

If a conservative 8% royalty rate had been charged on that $245 billion, we'd be almost $20 billion richer. And at that same 8% rate, the $3¾ billion in minerals that are currently being pulled out of public lands each year would earn the Treasury about $300 million a year.

A moratorium on mining claims has been declared while Congress tries to decide what to do about the Law of '72 (it's survived many challenges before, but maybe this time we'll be able to drive a golden stake through its heart). Of the approximately $34 billion in proven mineral reserves still left on public lands, 46% were in the process of being claimed when the moratorium went into effect.

But wait—there's more

The worst thing about the Law of '72 is that it doesn't require companies to clean up after themselves when they're done mining and return the patented land. Right now we're looking at cleanup costs of $32 to $72 billion for abandoned mines on public lands. Let's split the difference and say the cleanup costs $52 billion. If the cleanup takes twenty years, that will amount to $2.6 billion a year.

As if the Law of '72 weren't enough, mining companies enjoy a number of other tax write-offs. The reclamation deduction allows them to begin deducting the eventual closing costs of a mine as soon as it's opened, instead of when those costs actually occur. Needless to say, there's no requirement that the money the reclamation deduction saves the mining companies be set aside in a trust fund for the eventual reclamation of the mine. Eliminating this deduction would earn the Treasury about $40 million a year.

Mining companies can deduct 85% of the projected costs of exploring for certain minerals (finding the site, determining the quantity and quality of the minerals on it, and digging of shafts and tunnels) in the first year of mining, rather than over the life of the mine. And they can treat the sale of coal and iron as capital gains rather than as ordinary income.

These two tax loopholes cost us $135 million a year, but since they're already included in the totals for the accelerated depreciation and capital gains chapters, we won't count them again here.

The percentage depletion allowance
Finally, there's the percentage depletion allowance, another ancient law that's still on the books. It lets mining companies take a set percentage of the gross income they derive from a mine off their taxable incomes, and continue to do that for as long as that mine is producing. (Presumably this compensates them for the fact that they're depleting their source of income by mining it. Or did you think that the money they make *selling* the minerals was supposed to do that?)

The percentage depletion allowance varies depending on what's being mined; it ranges from 10% for clay, sand and gravel to 22% for uranium, sulphur and lead. (Note that some of the most toxic substances have the highest allowances.)

Just as with its twin, the oil depletion allowance, this tax break can end up being worth many times what it cost to dig the mine. When mining companies end up making more money from a tax write-off than they've invested in the mine, that means we've invested more in their mine than they have. Eliminating this allowance would save us $560 million a year.

Let's add things up. Royalty-free mining runs $300 million a year. Not requiring miners to clean up after themselves costs about $2.6 billion a year. The reclamation deduction runs $40 million a year and the percentage depletion allowance $560 million. That comes to a total of $3.5 billion a year (not including tax breaks we've counted elsewhere in the book).

OIL AND GAS TAX BREAKS

$2.4 BILLION A YEAR

Like the percentage depletion allowance just described, the *oil depletion allowance* lets certain companies deduct 15% of the gross income they derive from oil and gas wells from their taxable incomes, and continue to do that for as long as those wells are still producing. Some smaller companies get to increase the deduction by 1% for every dollar the price of oil falls below $20 a barrel.

This tax break, on which we lose about $1 billion a year, can add up to many times the cost of the original exploration and drilling. In fact, it formerly could amount to 100% of the company's profits—in which case the company paid no taxes, no matter how much money it made. Presently this is capped at 65% of profits.

The rationale for this loophole is that it encourages exploration for new oil—presumably something no oil company would otherwise do. Oil industry executives argue that other businesses are allowed to depreciate the costs of their manufacturing investments. That's true, but they're only allowed to take off the actual cost of those assets, not deduct 15% of their gross income virtually forever.

Introduced in 1926, the oil depletion allowance was restricted in 1975 to independent oil companies that don't refine or import oil. To make up for this, the larger, integrated companies were given the *intangible drilling cost deduction*, which in some ways is even better.

It lets them deduct 70% of the cost of setting up a drilling operation in the year those expenses occur, rather than having to depreciate them over the expected life of the well. The other 30% they can take off over the next five years. This boondoggle costs us about $500 million a year.

A third tax break is the *enhanced oil recovery credit*. It encourages oil companies to go after reserves that are more expensive to extract—

like those that have nearly been depleted, or that contain especially thick crude oil. The net effect of this credit, which costs us $500 million a year, is that we pay almost twice as much for gasoline made from domestic oil as we do for gas made from foreign oil.

Together, these three loopholes sometimes exceed 100% of the value of the energy produced by that oil. In other words, it would be cheaper in some cases for the government to just buy gasoline from the companies and give it to taxpayers free of charge.

(Of course, without the tax breaks, the oil companies would charge more for gasoline, bringing our prices closer to other countries'. This would undoubtedly lower our per capita consumption of gasoline, which is currently the highest in the world.)

There's a fourth tax break we can't count because we can't estimate its size; for details on it, see the section on "master limited partnerships" in the chapter called *What we've left out.* But miscellaneous smaller tax breaks and subsidies add an additional $400 million a year to the oil industry's wealthfare, which brings the total to $2.4 billion.

Instead of throwing $2.4 billion a year at the oil companies, we could encourage them to cut down on waste during production and transport. Each year, the equivalent of a thousand Exxon Valdez spills is lost due to inefficient refining, leaking wells and storage tanks, spills at oil fields and from tankers and pipelines, evaporative losses, unrecycled motor oil and the like.

The current oil and gas tax breaks encourage the use of fossil fuels at the expense of cleaner alternatives, reward drilling in environmentally sensitive areas like wetlands and estuaries, and artificially attract to the oil industry investment money that could be used more productively in other areas of the economy.

EXPORT SUBSIDIES

$2 BILLION A YEAR

Export subsidies take many forms. Under various programs—we won't bore you with all their names—the US Department of Agriculture (USDA) currently spends $1.1 *billion* a year helping US-based transnational corporations market their products abroad (and that figure is actually down from previous years).

These programs provide information on foreign markets, loans at below-market rates, funding for trade shows and advertising subsidies. (But, as Friends of the Earth points out, there's been little effort to assure that these funds actually increase overseas promotions, rather than simply pay for marketing the transnationals would be doing anyway.)

The USDA also provides "bonuses" to transnationals—many of them foreign firms—so that they can "sell US agricultural products in targeted countries at prices below the exporter's cost of acquiring them."

(When other countries do this to us, we call it "dumping" and protest vociferously.) Corporations that have benefited from the USDA's largess include (all figures are totals for 1985–94):

- Cargill (annual sales of $7 billion)—$1.3 billion
- Continental Grain (the fourth largest privately held corporation in the US, with sales of $15 billion)—$1.1 billion
- the US subsidiary of the French firm Louis Dreyfus (US sales of $1.7 billion)—$938 million
- Bunge Corp—$282 million
- the US subsidiary of the Italian firm Ferruzzi—$246 million
- Pillsbury—$163 million
- Mitsubishi USA—$114 million

Other struggling companies you were generous enough to subsidize: McDonald's, Dole, Sunkist, General Mills, Ernest & Julio Gallo, Campbell's Soup, Miller Beer, M&M Mars and American Legend (to help them peddle those mink coats overseas, where there's less chance paint will get thrown on them).

Beyond the USDA

There's almost another billion in export subsidies outside the USDA. The Export-Import Bank (Ex-Im), an independent agency that cost us $742 million (in fiscal 1996), provides low-interest loans and loan guarantees to foreign users of US products.

In 1994, for example, the murderous government of Indonesia got over $125 million in

Ex-Im loans to buy equipment from Hughes Aircraft (whose campaign contributions in the 1994 elections totalled $248,000). Other Ex-Im beneficiaries include needy corporations like GE and Boeing.

The Overseas Private Investment Corporation (OPIC) works the other side of the street. Instead of lending money to foreign governments and companies so they can buy US products, it spent $68 million (in fiscal 1996) financing US companies' investments in "developing" countries.

OPIC used to hand out a lot more money. In fiscal 1994, US West alone got $170 million in OPIC financing for projects in Russia and Hungary. (Just coincidentally, the company made $320,000 in campaign contributions that same year.)

Other 1994 OPIC welfare kings included Citibank ($388 million), Kimberly-Clark ($9.3 million) and Levi Strauss ($1.1 million). The last two companies were so happy with the overseas operations we financed that Kimberly-Clark transferred 600 jobs out of the US, and Levi Strauss transferred 100.

The State Department gives $125 million a year to foreign importers of US goods. And then there's the Pentagon. It runs several overseas loan programs, but since we've already discussed them in the chapter on military waste and fraud, we won't repeat ourselves here. Even without the Pentagon's programs, export subsidies total almost $2.4 billion a year.

SYNFUEL TAX CREDITS

$1.2 BILLION A YEAR

President Carter's synthetic fuels (synfuel) program, which aims to reduce dependence on imported oil, offers a tax credit for the production of synfuel from methane gas, shale, tar sands, coal and other fossil sources.

To some extent, this makes sense. An undisturbed coal deposit is normally laced with veins of methane; unless this methane is extracted beforehand, it escapes into the atmosphere while the coal is being mined.

It also makes sense to tap methane escaping from old garbage dumps and the like; it's a greenhouse gas, after all, and capturing it not only provides fuel but helps reduce global warming. (All synfuels—not just methane—come from fossil sources and contribute to the greenhouse effect.)

But it makes no sense to create artificial incentives to go after methane in risky areas where it would otherwise stay put, like old oil and gas fields. The new drilling fractures the earth and opens up new passageways; gas escapes through all kinds of holes besides the one just drilled (including old wells that weren't plugged properly); and drilling through a contaminated aquifer down into a pristine one contaminates the lower one.

This tax credit has encouraged synfuel production over conventional natural gas sources, which would otherwise be much cheaper. With oil prices relatively low, it hasn't saved consumers any money. What it has done—at a cost to us of almost $1.2 billion a year—is increase pollution, diminish interest in renewable energy solutions and enrich a few companies.

TIMBER SUBSIDIES

$427 MILLION A YEAR
(NOT COUNTING TAX BREAKS)

Here's a trivia question for you: What federal agency is responsible for the most miles of road in the US? The Department of Transportation? Nope. It's the US Forest Service, with 360,000 miles of logging roads—eight times more than the entire Interstate Highway System. The USFS continues to pay for thousands of miles more each year, at an annual cost of $95 million.

The Forest Service doesn't physically build the roads. Logging companies do, and the Forest Service pays for them by letting the companies cut down a certain number of trees. In order to barter like that, the USFS needs to decide how much each tree is worth.

Until recently, the prices were decided at secret meetings between Forest Service officials and timber industry executives. Although the Clinton administration did away with the secret meetings, the Forest Service is still stocked with big timber's cronies, and it continues to shamelessly undervalue our trees. Recently, it came up with a value of $2.85—the price of a cheeseburger—for a thousand board feet of lumber (about 1% of the normal commercial rate).

Just giving it away

In spite of prices like that, the Forest Service would like you to think they're making a profit managing our natural resources. They claim they made $214 million on timber sales in 1994, and $412 million in 1993. But that's only because they don't subtract a lot of their costs.

For example, they don't count what they pay the logging companies for new roads, which they say "add to the capital value of the forest." (Actually, logging roads contribute to soil erosion and water pollution, and to the loss of wildlife habitat and recreational value.)

The USFS also amortizes certain reforestation costs over extremely long time spans— sometimes as much as 400 years. When you look at the bottom line, you find that in 1994, the USFS lost $309 million; in 1993, $442 million; between 1985 and 1994, more than $5.6 billion.

As one economist has pointed out, "In terms of assets, the [USFS] would rank in the top five in *Fortune* magazine's list of the nation's 500 largest corporations. In terms of operating revenues, however, [it] would only be number 290. In terms of net income, [it] would be classified as bankrupt."

Of the 120 forests the USFS managed in 1994, 87% lost money. Nine lost money even before subtracting their costs! How is that possible? To answer that question, let's look at the biggest money-loser of all—the Tongass National Forest in Alaska.

Plundering the Tongass

The Tongass is the nation's largest forest and the largest remaining temperate rain forest on earth. A subsidiary of the giant conglomerate Louisiana Pacific (LP) has a contract with the USFS that guarantees it a 50-year monopoly on logging the Tongass at noncompetitive prices.

Recently, the value of the trees cut down by LP's subsidiary has been less than the cost of the roads it built, so we've been *paying* them millions of dollars a year—actually giving them checks—to cut down our trees!

In addition to being extremely beautiful, the Tongass hosts all five species of Pacific salmon, and the world's largest concentrations of grizzly bears and bald eagles. This doesn't impress Alaska's Republican senators, Ted Stevens and Frank Murkowski, who cosponsored legislation to increase logging operations in the Tongass by 48%.

That bill didn't pass, but a new one is even worse. It extends LP's lease to 2019 and *guarantees* that they make a profit in the Tongass for all that time. (Dave Katz of the Southeast Alaska Conservation Council calls it "the most egregious piece of corporate welfare I can imagine.")

This kind of thing is nothing new, unfortunately. Between 1987 and 1992, the timber industry contributed $6.9 million to congressional campaigns...and the USFS lost $1.5 *billion* on timber deals.

Special tax breaks

In addition to ripping off the Forest Service, the timber industry gets a bunch of lavish tax breaks. Since 1944, its income has been treated as capital gains, which is virtually always taxed at a lower rate than other types of income.

Timber companies are also allowed to deduct many capital costs up front (something other businesses can't do). A third tax loophole—the use of "master limited partnerships"—is discussed in the chapter called *What we left out.*

Because of these tax breaks, timber companies were deeply involved in the acquisitions, mergers and leveraged buyouts of the 1980s. This left many of them with huge debts; to pay the interest on them, they've been logging their own trees far faster than they can replace them. Now they have a huge appetite for more taxpayer-subsidized trees, and a crop of pliant politicians who are all too happy to give them what they want.

The timber industry's tax loopholes cost us about $520 million a year, but since they've already been counted in the accelerated depreciation and capital gains chapters, all we'll include here is the $95 million we pay for new logging roads each year, and the $332 million we lose by selling trees for less than they're worth.

OZONE TAX EXEMPTIONS

$320 MILLION A YEAR

In 1985, a hole in the earth's ozone layer was discovered over Antarctica, and it's been growing rapidly ever since. Ozone filters solar radiation, removing its most dangerous wavelengths; take ozone away and skin cancer rates skyrocket, as do many other ailments.

But the direct effects on human beings are the least of the problem. Most plant life evolved on earth under conditions of ozone-filtered solar radiation. If enough of that filtration is removed, you're looking at the death of virtually all plants...followed rapidly by the death of virtually all animals. It would be back to the drawing board—4.5 billion years back.

Alarmed by this threat, more than 120 nations agreed in 1987 to phase out the use of CFCs (chlorofluorocarbons) and several other ozone-destroying chemicals. In keeping with this international agreement—which is called the Montreal Protocol—Congress passed a tax on those chemicals in 1989. The tax has successfully discouraged their use, and has encouraged the development of safer substitutes.

Unfortunately, the story doesn't end there. A fumigant (gaseous pesticide) called methyl bromide was added to the Montreal Protocol in 1992. In addition to shredding the ozone layer, methyl bromide is a deadly poison. Farmworkers exposed to even tiny amounts of it often suffer seizures, cancer and respiratory ailments, and their children are born with birth defects. Larger doses damage the nervous system, often fatally.

Despite all that, methyl bromide still hasn't been added to the list of chemicals that pay the ozone-depletion tax. Why not? Because the Clinton administration agreed to leave it out in exchange for the support of 20 House members from California and Florida on the NAFTA treaty vote.

But wait—it gets worse. The 1990 Clean Air Act amendments require US companies to phase out production of methyl bromide by 2001, but the administration has been working hard to delay this ban to 2010, and to exempt "essential uses"—fumigation of strawberries, tomatoes and timber—even after that.

Since these "essential uses" are just about all methyl bromide is used for, the proposed exemptions have provoked angry opposition from Germany, Canada and the Netherlands, and environmental activists in the United States.

A class of chemicals called HCFCs— hydrochlorofluorocarbons—were also left out of the initial Montreal Protocol, so that they could provide a transition from the even more dangerous CFCs to safer substitutes. Alternatives have now been found for nearly every use of HCFCs (as well as CFCs), and HCFCs were added to the Montreal Protocol in 1992.

But our government continues to exempt them from the tax on ozone-depleting chemicals. Aside from costing us $320 million a year, this policy endangers every living thing on earth.

A BOUQUET OF MISCELLANEOUS RIP-OFFS

$1.6 BILLION A YEAR

Commercial ship subsidies • $1 billion a year
For agreeing to make their ships available to the US military in the event of a war, commercial ship owners are given an average annual subsidy of $3.5 million per ship. The Pentagon, which has more than enough ships of its own, admits this program serves no earthly purpose, but we still pay $1 billion a year for it. Perhaps the maritime industry's $17 million in PAC contributions over the past decade have something to do with it.

Fuel efficiency subsidies • $333 million a year
The government gives GM, Ford and Chrysler—whose combined 1994 profits were almost $14 billion—$333 million a year to develop more fuel-efficient cars. At the same time, the Big Three propagandize widely in favor of watered-down fuel-efficiency standards.

Advanced tech subsidies • $221 million a year
In fiscal 1996, the Commerce Department's Advanced Technology Program handed out $221 million in grants to the likes of GE,

IBM, United Airlines, Xerox and Du Pont, "to enhance the competitiveness" of these poor, hapless giants.

Taxol • $38 million a year

After the federal government spent fifteen years and $32 million discovering, developing and testing the anticancer drug Taxol, it gave Bristol-Myers Squibb (BMS) exclusive rights to market it, royalty-free. It costs BMS $52.50 to produce each shot of Taxol, which they then sell for $1,023! (That's wholesale, not retail.)

In 1995, BMS made $480 million on the drug. (That's profits, not sales.) If the government charged a conservative 8% royalty rate, it would be making more than $38 million on Taxol each year, instead of nothing. Why doesn't it? Because it never does.

Instead, it's relied on the "reasonable pricing" rule, which requires pharmaceutical firms not to overcharge for drugs developed with government assistance. Unfortunately, the Department of Health and Human Services dropped that rule in April 1995 (under heavy lobbying), which left BMS and other pharmaceutical companies free to charge whatever they want for government-developed drugs.

There are hundreds of such drugs, and the $38 million we lose on Taxol is a tiny fraction of what this no-royalty policy costs us each year. (What we don't understand is, where do they get the nerve to call themselves "ethical" drug companies?)

WHAT WE'VE LEFT OUT

UNTOLD BILLIONS EVERY YEAR

As we mentioned in the introduction, there are lots of types of wealthfare we couldn't list above. Although they're obviously treasure-troves of welfare for the rich, getting good figures for the wealthfare portion of them wasn't feasible (in some cases, it's virtually impossible, no matter how much time you have). In this chapter, we discuss a few of these areas, in no particular order.

State and local corporate welfare
Virtually all the wealthfare we've discussed so far in this book operates at the federal level, but state and local governments also slather benefits on companies within their borders, and many desperately compete for new corporate business—relocating factories, say—by handing out tax breaks and waiving environmental regulations. This is called "the race to the bottom."

You can probably think of an example in your area—maybe a sports team that threatened to leave town unless the city built them a new stadium. Here are some of the worst of these deals from 1994:

- Baton Rouge, Louisiana gave Exxon a $14.4-million tax break in exchange for a net gain of exactly one job (by Exxon's own projections). Almost 75% of Louisiana's property tax exemptions go to projects that create no new permanent jobs.

- Blue Water Fibre accepted $81 million in aid from three state agencies in Michigan to build a recycling mill. Building the mill created 200 temporary jobs, 170 of which went to out-of-state workers. Running the mill created 34 permanent jobs—at a cost of $2.4 million each.

- In return for creating just 30 permanent jobs, Methanol One took tax breaks from Alabama worth between $300,000 and $3.3 million per job created.

- When Ipsco, a Canadian firm, planned to build a new steel mill that would employ 300 workers, it gave the Iowa legislature eleven days to decide on a $73-million package. The lawmakers missed the deadline but forked over the cash anyway. (How could they resist, at just $243,000 per job?)

One North Carolina citizen was so outraged by the wasteful expenditure of city and county funds for 24 separate "economic incentive projects" that he sued, arguing that the law authorizing such grants violated the state's constitution. The Superior Court ruled in his favor but, in March 1996, the North Carolina Supreme Court overruled.

Easy treatment of white-collar criminals

Although much of what we've already discussed in this book can be considered white-collar crime, there's also a lot of it we haven't covered. That's what this section is about.

The easy treatment white-collar criminals get in this country isn't a spending program or a tax break, but it is a form of welfare for the rich. When the fines imposed by the EPA, for example, are so low that polluting companies consider them a normal cost of doing business (along with the tax-deductible cost of the lawyers they use to defend themselves against the charges), we end up paying, both in higher health care costs and higher cleanup costs.

All the burglaries, robberies and muggings in the US cost us about $4 billion in 1995. That same year, crime in the suites, perpetrated by corporate officers, lawyers, accountants, doctors and the like, cost us *$200 billion*—50 times as much. This figure, which comes from W. Steve Albrecht, a professor of accountancy at Brigham Young University, includes the costs of fraud, defective products, monopolistic practices and the like, but it doesn't include pollution costs, governmental corruption or preventable on-the-job deaths due to negligence.

No one knows how much money is stolen from the medical system each year, but estimates range up to $250 billion—25% of the trillion dollars spent each year. But that's just money. While there are 24,000 murders in the US each year, medical negligence kills an estimated *80,000* of us—more than three times as many.

On-the-job accidents and occupational diseases like black lung or asbestosis kill 56,000 people each year—more than twice as many as are murdered. (It's estimated that nearly a third of all cancer deaths are due to carcinogens in the workplace.) Another 28,000 people die each year from dangerous or defective products, and 130,000 more are injured.

Air-bag technology has been around since the early 1970s, but for twenty years the auto industry fought efforts to enact a federal law requiring air bags as standard equipment on new cars. Now they tout them in their advertising. In the meantime, an estimated *140,000* of the people who lost their lives in accidents in those twenty years would still be alive if their cars had been equipped with air bags.

Asbestos, banned since 1975, is *still* killing 8000 Americans a year. The list goes on and on and on. Yet virtually all we hear about in the media is the supposedly heavy regulatory burden imposed on US industry. Some burden. Of all the cases the Justice Department prosecutes, those involving product safety, occupational diseases and environmental crimes combined amount to $\frac{1}{2}$ of 1%.

Horse write-offs

The original idea behind the tax deduction for horse expenses was that horses were essential to the functioning of a farm, like pigs and cattle. Although that's no longer true for most of the horses in this country, this deduction has been expanded into a major tax shelter.

As the *Wall Street Journal* put it, "some of the people breeding horses now...can barely tell a horse from a donkey, but [they] recognize a nice tax shelter." And they aren't too subtle about it either, as you can see from some of the names given racehorses in recent years: My Deduction, Tax Dodge, Tax Gimmick, Write Off, My Write Off, Another Shelter and Justa Shelter.

If you own a horse, you can deduct the costs of food, housing, vet bills, stud fees, transportation, insurance, interest charges, depreciation, attendance at horse shows, visits to horse farms, and state and local taxes.

Wilhelmina du Pont Ross, a member of one of the wealthiest families in the world, hired her husband to run their stables and wrote off his salary on their joint tax return. Her relative, William du Pont, Jr., whose vast estate in Maryland contained a grandstand that could seat 12,500 people, deducted the cost of keeping professional foxhunters on staff.

You can trade an older horse for one that's younger and more valuable without paying any taxes on the exchange. And when you sell a horse, the profit is taxed at the lower capital gains rate, rather than as ordinary income. If you don't want the bother of actually owning horses, leasing programs allow you to cash in on the tax advantages, without any unpleasant odors on the estate.

All of this is kept in place by the vigorous lobbying of the American Horse Council, whose representatives virtually write the laws in this area. There isn't much opposition to these loopholes, both because most people don't know about them and because everybody loves horses. (Of course, it isn't the *horses* who get the tax breaks.)

Cut-rate electricity
In 1935, the government set out to bring electricity—and later, telephone service—to

rural America. This mission was largely completed 40 years ago; nearly 100% of rural America now has electricity, and 98% has telephone service—better numbers than the nation as a whole.

In spite of that, various government agencies continue to provide about $2 billion a year in grants, subsidized loans and below-market electricity to profitable utilities—some with sales in the billions. Some of the areas these utilities service—like Las Vegas—can hardly be considered rural anymore.

The Northeast is the only region of the country not served by these programs; not coincidentally, it has the highest power costs in the nation. This accounts for a great deal of job flight, as manufacturing firms relocate to areas with subsidized power. In effect, Northeastern taxpayers shell out tax money so their jobs can be moved to Tennessee or Idaho.

Some electricity subsidies provide low-cost power to schools, hospitals and Indian reservations. But they also subsidize businesses like casinos and ski resorts that benefit from cheap power. So the next time you find yourself bathed in the ghastly glare of Las Vegas, you can tell yourself proudly, "I paid for that."

In 1995, Senator John McCain (R–Arizona) introduced legislation to means-test the recipients of these programs, but it was defeated. As a result, we can't estimate how much of these subsidies amount to welfare for the rich.

Miscellaneous corporate tax breaks

Some economists make the following argument: Since corporations always pass their costs along to their customers, consumers ultimately pay all corporate taxes. Thus there's really no such thing as corporate taxation.

If this were true, then the lower the corporate tax rate, the higher consumer spending power would be. In the real world, however, the opposite is often the case.

In the 1950s, when the corporate tax rate was 52% and corporations paid almost a third of all income taxes, a single wage earner could support a family of four and could afford a new house, a car and major appliances. In the 1990s, when the corporate tax rate ranges between 15% and 39% and corporations pay less than 10% of all income taxes, more than half of all families have two or more wage earners and businesses are laying off people left and right.

(According to the US Bureau of Labor Statistics, average earnings of nonsupervisory workers peaked in 1973, and they've been going down ever since. By 1992, they were 12% lower than they were in 1965.)

So it seems that corporations *retain* some of the savings they get from lower tax rates— which isn't surprising, since they lobby so ferociously for them. Their investment in certain key legislators can be repaid many times over.

For example, section 543(b) of the US tax code contains a provision that applies only to corporations formed in Nevada on January

27, 1972. It allows Cantor, Fitzgerald & Co.— the only company incorporated in Nevada on that date—to exempt certain interest income involving securities and money-market funds from taxation.

Hand-crafted tax breaks like that are nothing new. Movie mogul Louis B. Mayer had a provision inserted into the Revenue Act of 1951 that classified his retirement package as capital gains rather than ordinary income. As a result, it was taxed at 20% instead of 90%, and he saved nearly $2 million in federal taxes.

Unlimited interest deductions
If you have to borrow money, either to make ends meet or to start a business, the interest you pay on that loan shouldn't be counted as part of your taxable income. That fair-minded principle was the basis for the deduction for interest payments. But by making the deduction virtually unlimited for corporations, Congress has subsidized a mountain of debt that's paid for by the average taxpayer.

In the 1950s, US corporations paid $185 billion in federal income tax; in the 1980s, they paid $675 billion—more than $3\frac{1}{2}$ times as much. In contrast, corporate interest payments rose from $44 billion in the 1950s to $2.2 trillion ($2,200 billion!) in the 1980s— 50 times as much. Thus in those thirty years, corporate interest has grown almost fourteen times faster than corporate taxes.

The interest deduction on corporate debt currently costs us over $200 billion a year. Once this deduction subsidized the replacement of plants and equipment or the hiring of new workers, but it increasingly underwrites the shuffling of paper assets.

The absence of limits on this write-off helped fuel the great financial scams of the 1980s, like the S&L scandal, the rise of junk bonds and the mania for mergers and acquisitions. Between 1980 and 1988, US companies spent over two-thirds of a trillion dollars buying each other in mergers and acquisitions. In the case of leveraged buyouts— which are financed by borrowing large sums of money—the resulting debt-ridden companies were forced to lay off workers and sell productive assets to pay off their creditors.

None of this created a single additional product, but it did create staggeringly huge fortunes. The unlimited interest deduction helped them do that, by subsidizing the borrowing that made the layoffs and selloffs necessary.

It still seems fair to keep interest payments deductible for most taxpayers. But we don't think any company should be allowed to deduct interest payments that exceed its income.

Master limited partnerships

Another corporate tax break is the master limited partnership, or MLP, which allowed even large corporations like Burger King and Days Inn to restructure as partnerships. Why would they want to do that? Because profits parceled out to the partners are taxed just on their individual income tax returns. So by restructuring as an MLP, a corporation can pay the same dividends as always to its investors, but avoid paying taxes on them at the corporate level.

From 1981 to 1987, there was nothing limited about these master limited partnerships; they cost the Treasury more than $500 million a year. This loophole was plugged in 1987, but with an exception—MLPs are still allowed in the oil, gas and timber industries. So Burlington Industries was able to take a timber corporation that paid corporate taxes of $33 million in 1988, and turn it into an MLP that paid no taxes at all in 1989.

Low-cost labor

In 1968, one person working full-time at the minimum wage would come pretty close to the federal poverty level for a family of four (so if someone else in the family worked just part-time, that family would be over the poverty line). Today that same full-time, minimum-wage job takes a worker up to just 56% of the poverty line.

Who makes up the difference? We do, through food stamps, the Earned Income Tax Credit and other programs designed to help the working poor. In effect, we're subsidizing employers so that they can pay less than a living wage.

The Federal Reserve Board tries to keep the pool of unemployed workers above 5%, so as not to fuel inflation. (It does that by raising or lowering interest rates to slow down or speed up the economy.) Unemployment above 5% guarantees that there will be plenty of competition for jobs at below-subsistence wages. But there's a steadily growing pool of even cheaper labor—the nation's prison population.

Prison labor

Since 1990, thirty states have legalized contracting prison labor to private firms. Inmates are now employed booking reservations for TWA, doing data entry for the Bank of America and restocking shelves for Toys "R" Us. Not only do prisoners work for much lower wages than people on the outside, but they have virtually no way to organize or strike. For an employer, it's the best of all possible worlds.

The US imprisons more of its citizens than any other nation on earth, and prison construction is growing by leaps and bounds. This great boon to the construction industry results from mandatory minimums for nonviolent drug offenders, the tough new "three-strikes" laws—the California version alone is costing $5.5 billion a year, five times what was estimated—and the roundup of illegal aliens.

In fact, as of 1995, the largest employer of illegal aliens in the US was Unicor, a $500 million-a-year company that pays prison laborers between 23¢ and $1.15 an hour to make clothing and furniture for the US government.

Automobile subsidies

Automobiles kill about 50,000 of us each year, nearly as many as died in the entire

Vietnam War. Respiratory diseases caused by auto exhaust kill another 120,000 Americans prematurely every year; their medical bills run more than $100 billion. Traffic injuries and deaths cost $400 billion a year.

Crop losses and property damage from car pollution (like damage to buildings caused by acid rain) cost another $100 billion a year. Motor vehicle fees and US gasoline taxes—the lowest in the industrialized world—don't begin to cover these costs; they're paid by drivers and nondrivers alike, and by future generations of taxpayers.

Cars offer convenience, privacy and safety. These are important benefits, but if the true costs of using a car were reflected in vehicle prices, registration fees, gas prices, etc., a lot more people would choose public transportation, bicycling and walking than do today.

Federal, state and local governments spend over $300 billion a year—nearly a hundred times what they spend on public transportation—on car-related costs like road construction and maintenance, enforcement of traffic laws, and the like. Riders on Amtrak and local mass transit systems pay much more towards their cost than auto users do—and at much less cost to society.

According to one estimate (which adds things like worktime lost because of traffic jams), the true social cost of automobiles to US society is *$1.4 trillion a year*—and that's *beyond* what we pay, as individuals and businesses, to buy and use them. If none of these costs were subsidized, hidden away or ignored, cars would cost more than $200,000 *apiece.*

Now, most people own cars, and some of these subsidies benefit as well as harm us. But $1.4 trillion is a lot of money, and it includes huge handouts to the oil companies, the car manufacturers, the mining companies (who supply the raw materials that are turned into a new car every second) and the road construction industry (which has paved over 38 million acres of our meadows, forests and plains). Automobile subsidies have also been a great boon to the real estate industry, as the Interstate Highway System and other roads made vast tracts of land more accessible.

The extent to which automobiles dominate our lives didn't just happen by accident—at least part of it was the result of a criminal conspiracy. Back in the early 1930s, most people living in cities got around on electric streetcars. Concerned that this wasn't the kind of environment in which they could sell a lot of buses, General Motors, using a series of front companies, began buying up streetcar systems, tearing out the tracks, buying buses from itself and then selling the new, polluting bus systems back to the cities—usually with contracts that prohibited purchase of "any new equipment using fuel or means of propulsion other than gas." Sometimes the contracts required that the new owners buy all their replacement buses from GM.

GM was soon joined by Greyhound, Firestone Tire and Rubber, Standard Oil of California (also called Chevron) and Mack Trucks. In 1949—after these companies had destroyed more than 100 streetcar systems in more than 45 cities, including New York, Los Angeles, Philadelphia, San Francisco, Oakland, Baltimore, St. Louis and Salt Lake City—GM, Chevron and Firestone were convicted of a criminal conspiracy to restrain trade.

They were fined $5000 each and the executives who organized the scheme were fined $1 each. (Ouch! They'll certainly never do anything like *that* again.)

The legacy of this conspiracy lives on. If you seek a monument to it, look above you. In the 1930s, when LA had the world's largest interurban electric railway system, the air over the city was clean every day of the year.

Other categories

Here are some other scams and tax breaks we couldn't get good wealthfare figures for: Medicare waste and fraud; the effects of Federal Reserve policies; the NAFTA and GATT treaties; the deregulation of various industries; import restrictions against Asian computer parts (which are said to add enormously to what US consumers pay for personal computers); fraudulent charitable deductions; and depreciation of real property (which—since it tends to increase, not decrease, in value—shouldn't be depreciated at all).

There are many other types of wealthfare, but by now you've surely gotten the point: our federal, state and local governments have become so corrupt that dispensing welfare to corporations and wealthy individuals has become their major activity. The only time they do anything for average citizens is when we force them to.

_____

WHAT YOU CAN DO ABOUT ALL THIS

The long litany of scams and ripoffs we've presented has probably got you pretty discouraged. But there is hope. For starters, everybody's already *against* welfare for the rich, and that's more than you can say about most political issues. Wealthfare can't stand the light of day; once it's seen for what it is, there's enormous pressure to eliminate it.

That's why the infamous oil depletion allowance, which used to be unlimited, is now capped at 65% of profits. (Yes, we know, but the journey of a thousand miles begins with a single step.)

The deduction for business meals and entertainment has been cut in half. The capital gains tax rate is still lower than the rate for ordinary income, but the gap is smaller than it has been for most of the last 75 years.

Although still grotesque, military waste and fraud is probably less obscene than it was a few years ago. The deductible on the nuclear industry's catastrophe insurance has been raised from $560 million to $7 billion, and two enormous nuclear boondoggle programs were killed in 1994 and 1995.

So don't despair—there's plenty we can do to reduce wealthfare. Basically, we need to show how pervasive it is, and suggest ways to eliminate it. There are at least four approaches to the problem:

- take politicians off the auction block
- make taxes fairer
- give the media back to the people
- stop letting the military scare us

We'll discuss each of these goals in turn, and provide contact information for groups that are working toward them. Then we'll list groups that attack wealthfare on several different fronts, and legislation that's attempting to reduce it.

The best government money can buy

As long as politicians need a lot of money to get elected, they'll be in the pockets of the people who pay to get them elected (at least most of them will). We can fight like hell to kill one or another ridiculous pork-barrel subsidy or loophole, and we may succeed from time to time, but until we reform campaign financing, some new form of wealthfare is sure to replace the old one.

In most European countries, all national-level political campaigns are substantially financed by the government. Doing that here would be enormously expensive, you say? Not as expensive as continuing to shovel almost half a trillion dollars a year at the corporate forces that control our political system.

130

Besides, the major expense of a modern political campaign is television advertising, and we own the airwaves (or at least we're supposed to). If broadcasters were required to provide airtime to candidates free of charge, campaigns would cost a small fraction of what they do now.

One group that's been focussing very strongly on this issue is Common Cause (for contact information, see the *General organizations* section below). Common Cause supported S1219, a campaign finance measure introduced by Senators John McCain (R–Arizona) and Russell Feingold (D–Wisconsin) and cosponsored by seventeen other senators from both parties. S1219 garnered the votes of more than half the Senate, but it couldn't reach the 60% supermajority needed to cut off the filibuster that was pitted against it.

Still, if the issue of campaign finance reform can bring McCain and Feingold together from opposite sides of the political spectrum, there's some reason to be hopeful—especially if we vote out of office any senator who didn't support S1219. To help you do that, here's a list of the senators who voted against it (all are Republicans except Howell Heflin):

Up for reelection in 1996: Thad Cochran (MS), Larry Craig (ID), Pete Domenici (NM), Sheila Frahm (KS), Phil Gramm (TX), Jesse Helms (NC), James Inhofe (OK), Mitch McConnell (KY), Larry Pressler (SD), Robert Smith (NH), Ted Stevens (AK), Strom Thurmond (SC), John Warner (VA).

Up for reelection in 1998: Robert Bennett (UT), Christopher Bond (MO), Ben Nighthorse Campbell (CO), Dan Coats (IN), Paul Coverdell (GA), Alfonse D'Amato (NY), Lauch Faircloth (NC), Charles Grassley (IA), Judd Gregg (NH), Kay Hutchinson (TX), Dick Kempthorne (ID), Frank Murkowski (AK), Don Nickles (OK), Richard Shelby (AL).

Up for reelection in 2000: Spencer Abraham (MI), John Ashcroft (MO), Conrad Burns (MT), John Chafee (RI), Mike DeWine (OH), Bill Frist (TN), Slade Gorton (WA), Rod Grams (MT), Orrin Hatch (UT), Jon Kyl (AZ), Trent Lott (MS), Richard Lugar (IN), Connie Mack (FL), William Roth (DE), Rick Santorum (PA), Craig Thomas (WY).

Retiring in 1996: Hank Brown (CO), Mark Hatfield (OR), Howell Heflin (AL).

The House had a similar campaign finance reform bill—HR2566, the Bipartisan Clean Congress Act—which was cosponsored by Representatives Linda Smith (R–Washington), Marty Meehan (D–New York) and Chris Shays (R–Connecticut). Like S1219, it imposed spending limits on campaigns, restricted out-of-state and special-interest money, closed loopholes and strengthened enforcement of election laws.

Both S1219 and HR2566 are in legislative limbo—neither was ever brought to the floor for a vote. They may be resurrected in future sessions of Congress; if not, similar bills will be introduced. The main danger is phony proposals like Newt Gingrich's, which actually *raised* the overall campaign contribution limit (fortunately, this bill was voted down). Your

best bet is to contact Common Cause to see
what bills they're currently supporting.

Tax fairness

There are lots of proposals out there for making our taxes simpler. Unfortunately, few of
them will make them *fairer*. (Just making
them fairer will automatically make them
simpler—as well as reduce them for 99% of
the population.) Of the groups working
toward that goal, two of the best are:

Citizens for Tax Justice, 1311 L St NW, Washington
   DC 20005 • phone: 202 626 3780 • website:
   http://www.ctj.org. They have a report on unfair
   tax breaks called *The Hidden Entitlements*.

Taxpayers for Common $ense, 651 Pennsylvania
   Ave SE, 2nd flr, Washington DC 20003 • phone:
   202 546 8500 • fax: 202 546 8511 • e-mail
   staff@taxpayer.net • website: http://www.tax-
   payer.net/~taxpayer/index.html.

*Important note: Don't type in the periods after web-
site addresses, or hyphens at the ends of lines.*

Don't like the media? Become the media

We find Noam Chomsky's analysis quite convincing: "The major media are large corporations, owned by and interlinked with even
larger conglomerates. Like other corporations,
they sell a product to a market. The market is
advertisers—that is, other businesses. The
product is audiences, [and] for the elite
media, [they're] relatively privileged audiences. So we have major corporations selling
fairly wealthy and privileged audiences to

other businesses. Not surprisingly, the picture of the world presented reflects the narrow and biased interests and values of the
sellers, the buyers and the product."

For that reason, we believe we'll be a lot
better off creating new media of our own,
rather than trying to reform the corporate-
owned ones—particularly if we want them to
carry hard-hitting stories about corporate
welfare. Here are some organizations that
facilitate alternative media:

The **Institute for Alternative Journalism** hosts the
annual Media and Democracy Congress, the first
of which was held in San Francisco in March
1996. IAJ is located at 77 Federal St, San Francisco CA 94107 • phone: 415 284 1420 • fax: 415
284 1414 • e-mail: alternet@igc.apc.org
• website: http://www.alternet.org/an/.

Media Watchdog is a website with links to far more
media activist groups than we could list here. It's
at http://theory.lcs.mit.edu/~mernst/media/.

The **Media Foundation** publishes the excellent
Adbusters magazine and has one of the coolest
websites around (http://www.adbusters.org/-
adbusters/main.html). They're at 1243 W 7th Ave,
Vancouver BC V6H 1B7 Canada • phone: 604
736 9401 • fax: 604 737 6021 • e-mail:
adbuster@wimsey.com.

FAIR (Fairness and Accuracy in Reporting) publishes a vital journal of media criticism called *Extra!*,
as well as numerous special reports and a syndi-
cated column. They also have a radio program.
They're at 130 W 25th St, New York NY 10001

WHAT YOU CAN DO ABOUT ALL THIS

- phone: 212 633 6700 • fax: 212 727 7668
- e-mail: fair@igc.apc.org • website: http://-www.fair.org/fair/.

TJ Walker presents his **Media Guerrilla Warfare Handbook for Liberals** online at http://www.idir.-net/~liberals. It offers great advice on staging media events, holding press conferences and sending out press releases, speaking in sound bites, getting on talk radio and even getting your own talk show.

The **Alliance for Community Media** runs conferences and video festivals, publishes a directory of organizations, and engages in advocacy and litigation. (This section's subhead is paraphrased from the headline of one of their ads; ultimately, it comes from Scoop Nisker's immortal "if you don't like the news, go out and make some of your own.") ACM's national office is at 666 11th St NW, Suite 806, Washington DC 20001
- phone: 202 393 2650 • fax: 202 393 2653
- e-mail: acm@alliancecm.org.

The **Alliance for Cultural Democracy**, an international organization headquartered in San Francisco, publishes a quarterly called *Cultural Democracy*. They can be reached at Box 192244, San Francisco CA 94119 • phone: 415 821 9652 or 415 437 2721 • e-mail: acd@f8.com *or* cdemocracy@aol.com • website: http://www.-f8.com/ACD/.

The wages of fear

If you take just one thought away from this book, let it be this: Military waste and fraud accounts for 40% of all welfare for the rich—far more than any other category. Any politician

135

who talks about ending corporate welfare, or balancing the budget, without proposing to cut Pentagon expenditures *at least 25–50%* is a charlatan.

This isn't just an economic issue. Since military waste and fraud make our country weaker, not stronger, eliminating them is also a matter of national security. Here are some of the best groups working on the problem:

The **Center for Defense Information**, 1500 Massachusetts Ave NW, Washington DC 20005
  • phone: 202 862 0700 • e-mail: info@cdi.org
  • website: http://www.cdi.org/

The **Defense Budget Project**, 777 N Capitol St NE, Suite 710, Washington DC 20002 • phone: 202 408 1517 • fax: 202 408 1526 • e-mail: dbp@cap.gwu.edu

The **Federation of American Scientists**, 307 Massachusetts Ave SE, Washington DC 20002
  • phone: 202 546 3300 • fax: 202 675 1010
  • e-mail: fas@fas.org

The **Friends Committee for National Legislation**, 245 Second St NE, Washington DC 20002
  • phone: 202 547 6000 • fax: 202 547 6019
  • e-mail: fcnl@igc.apc.org

20/20 Vision, 1828 Jefferson Pl NW, Washington DC 20036 • phone: 202 833 2020 • fax: 202 833 5307 • e-mail: vision@igc.apc.org

The **War Resisters League**, 339 Lafayette St, New York NY 10012 • phone: 212 228 0450 • fax: 212 228 6193 • e-mail: wrl@igc.apc.org

Also see the **PeaceNet** listing in *Recommended reading* (p. 142).

General organizations

Several organizations attack corporate welfare—and other injustices—on more than
one front. This section lists some of the best
of them. (More groups are discussed in *Recommended reading*, which comes right after
this chapter.)

As we've mentioned, **Common Cause** has been
    mounting a major campaign against corporate
    welfare and for campaign finance reform. You
    can reach them at 2030 M St NW, Washington
    DC 20036 • phone: 202 833 1200 • fax: 202
    659 3716.

The **Corporate Welfare Project** (started by Ralph
    Nader) is run by Janice Shields out of the offices
    of the Public Interest Research Group, 218 D St
    SE, Washington DC 20003 • phone: 202 546
    9707 • e-mail: jshields@essential.org • website:
    http://www.csrl.org/ is.

Public Citizen (also started by Ralph Nader) is at
    1600 20th St NW, Washington DC 20009
    • phone: 202 588 1000 • fax: 202 588 7799
    • e-mail: pnye@citizen.org.

The **Share the Wealth Project** has a Corporate Wel-
    fare Organizing Kit and other resources. It's locat-
    ed at 37 Temple Pl, 5th flr, Boston MA 02111
    • phone 617 423 2148 • fax 617 695 1295
    • e-mail: stw19@nfi.com • website: http://-
    www.stw.org/.

Anti-wealthfare legislation

As described at the beginning of this chapter,
Senators John McCain (R–Arizona) and Russell Feingold (D–Wisconsin)—that ideological
odd couple—introduced a strong campaign

finance reform bill. They also introduced S1376, which proposes setting up a bipartisan corporate welfare commission.

Cosponsoring S1376 are Senators Edward Kennedy and John Kerry (both D–Massachusetts), Fred Thompson (R–Tennessee) and Dan Coats (R–Indiana). As you can see, they come from both parties and have widely varying political views, so this really isn't a partisan issue. If your senators don't support this bill, replace them with ones who will.

There's also anti-wealthfare legislation in the House. HR2534, the Corporate Responsibility Act, was introduced by Representative Bernie Sanders (I–Vermont) and cosponsored by Representatives John Conyers (D–Michigan), Maurice Hinchey (D–New York), Cynthia McKinney (D–Georgia), Eleanor Holmes Norton (D–Washington, DC), Martin Meehan and John Olver (both D–Massachusetts), Major Owens (D–New York), and Carlos Romero-Barcelo (D–Puerto Rico).

HR2534 proposes an alternative budget that cuts more than $100 billion a year in corporate subsidies and tax breaks. A draft of the bill is available from the Electronic Policy Network (Box 383080, Cambridge MA 02238 • phone: 617 547 2950 • e-mail: query@epn.org), or you can view a synopsis of it online at http://epn.org/prospect/library/bcbudg.html.

HR2534 exists in legislative limbo, because Newt Gingrich and Dick Armey won't let it come to the floor for a vote.

Each year, an alternative budget—similar but not identical to HR2534—is proposed by the Congressional Black Caucus and the House Progressive Caucus. Their alternative budgets for fiscal 1996 and 1997 have already been voted down.

Is debt a bad thing?

Before we end, we'd like to make one last point. As this book goes to press, the Clinton administration and the GOP-dominated Congress are trying to cut the deficit by about $1.4 trillion over seven years.

In a budget as riddled with fat as ours, that's easy to do—just cut our elephantine Pentagon expenditures and you're done. But of course they're just using the *idea* of eliminating the deficit as an excuse for cutting certain programs that merely help people, rather than generate campaign contributions.

This sudden desire to balance the budget, after running record deficits during the Reagan/Bush years, is rationalized by saying that every family and business balances its checkbook, so why can't Uncle Sam? Leaving aside the fact that lots of people couldn't balance their checkbooks if their lives depended on it, virtually every family also borrows large sums of money for things like home mortgages, car loans and the cost of college educations, and any successful business carries significant debt as well.

If every US household and business eliminated all its debt, economic activity in this country would grind to a halt. The same thing would happen if the federal government stopped borrowing. Reasonable amounts of indebtedness are an investment in the future (and our national debt *is* reasonable—as a percentage of GDP, it's smaller than the debt of virtually every other industrialized country).

Not using public debt to invest in roads, bridges, education, research, public health measures, etc. etc. is extremely short-sighted—and virtually unheard-of among the nations of the world. On the other hand, *half* of our $5 trillion debt comes from military pork and tax breaks for the rich that the government wasted our money on just during the Reagan/Bush years, and virtually the only effect of all that was to increase income disparity and weaken the country.

Which brings us back to the main point of this book: It's not hard to balance the budget, if that's what we really want to do. All we have to do is take the rich off welfare.

RECOMMENDED READING

Reports

The Progressive Policy Institute has an online synopsis of their report *Cut and Invest* at http://www.dlcppi.org/library.htm. Or you can order the full report from PPI at 518 C Street NE, Washington DC 20002 • phone: 202 547 0001 • fax: 202 544 5014.

CUTS (Citizens United to Trim Subsidies) is a coalition of many groups, including Friends of the Earth. It has two reports on welfare for polluters, which can be viewed online: **The Green Scissors Report** (http://www.foe.org/scissors96/) and **Dirty Little Secrets** (http://www.foe.org/dsl.html). You can get hard copies of these reports from Public Interest Publications, 800 537 9359.

Another good report is **The Zero Deficit Plan**, available online or on paper from the Concord Coalition, 1019 19th St NW, Suite 810, Washington DC 20036 • phone: 202 467 6222 • website: http://www.texas.net/users/andyn/zdpindex.html.

The conservative Cato Institute has two reports that can be viewed online: **Ending Corporate Welfare as We Know It** (http://www.cato.org/pubs/pas/-pa225es.html) and **How Corporate Welfare Won** (http://www.cato.org/pubs/pas/pa~254es.html). You can also order hard copies from Cato at 1000 Massachusetts Ave NW, Washington DC 20001 • phone: 202 842 0200 • fax: 202 842 3490 • e-mail: cato@cato.org. (The Cato Institute has done some fine work on corporate welfare, but we don't necessarily agree with anything else they stand for.)

There's a lot of useful stuff in the annual **Pig Book** put out by Citizens Against Government Waste (1301 Connecticut Ave NW, Suite 400, Washington DC 20036). Part of it's available online at http://www.govt-waste.org, or you can order the whole book from 1 800 BE ANGRY.

For some clear analysis of welfare for the poor, Katha Pollitt of *The Nation* recommends **Welfare Myths: Fact or Fiction**, $10 from the Center on Social Welfare Policy and Law, 275 Seventh Ave #1205, New York NY 10001 • phone: 212 633 6967.

Online information

PeaceNet is run by the Institute for Global Communications, which also runs EcoNet and LaborNet. IGC is at 18 Deboom St, San Francisco CA 94107 • phone: 415 442 0220 • fax: 415 561 6101 • e-mail: outreach@igc.org • website: http://www.igc.org.

Ralph Nader's **Essential Information**, which is an umbrella group for his other organizations, runs an excellent website at http://www.essential.org/.

Several other fine websites deal with this issue:

Charlotte's Web Corporate Welfare Page, at http://emf.net/~cr/corp-welfare.html

Great Moments in Corporate Welfare, at http://-www.lm.com/~ukeith/welfare.html

Rachel's Corporate Welfare Information Center, at http://www.envirolink.org/issues/corporate/-welfare/index.html

Utne Reader's Corporate Welfare Resources, at http://www.utnereader.com:80/archive/lens01/-exchange/1naderres.html (good God—that's the longest website address we've ever seen!)

Websites that deal with specific aspects of the problem of corporate welfare are listed elsewhere in this appendix, and also in various sections of the *What you can do about all this* chapter.

Periodicals

We find *The Nation* the best general source for information on wealthfare and many other outrages, as well as for some of the best political writing around. Any decent newsstand carries it, but if you can't find it, they're at 72 Fifth Ave, New York NY 10011 • phone: 212 242 8400.

Russell Mokhiber's weekly **Corporate Crime Reporter** is full of valuable information, but it's quite expensive. Get your library to order it (from Box 18384, Washington DC 20036 • phone: 202 737 1680); if they won't, any good law school library should have it. (Mokhiber has also written an excellent book. See the next section for details.)

Z magazine is also worthwhile, especially since it's the best place to find Noam Chomksy's latest writings. *Z* is located at 18 Millfield St, Woods Hole MA 02543 • phone: 508 548 9063 • fax: 508 547 0626 • e-mail: Lydia_Sargent@lbbs.org • website: http://www.lbbs.org.

Despite its name, **Covert Action Quarterly** doesn't just cover the so-called "intelligence community." It also has articles on white-collar crime and other abuses, and frequently publishes Noam Chomsky. *CAQ* is at 1500 Massachusetts Ave NW, #732, Washington DC 20005 • phone: 202 331 9763 • fax: 202 331 9751 • e-mail: caq@igc.apc.org • website: http://www.worldmedia.com/caq.

Mother Jones is useful too. It's available at most newsstands, but you can contact them directly at 731 Market St, Suite 600, San Francisco CA 94103 • phone: 415 665 6637 • fax 415 665 6696 • e-mail: backtalk@mojones.com • website http://www.mojones.com.

The Progressive publishes a lot of valuable stuff. It's at 409 E Main St, Madison WI 53703 • phone: 608 257 4626.

Joel Bleifuss of **In These Times** has done some good work on wealthfare. *ITT* is at 2040 N Milwaukee Ave, Chicago IL 60647 • phone: 312 772 0100 • e-mail itt@igc.apc.org.

Earth Island Journal is the monthly magazine of
Earth Island Institute. Edited by the amazing Gar
Smith, *EIJ* has broken so many important stories
that it must hold some kind of record. Although
the magazine's focus is environmental, it follows
up on the money angle whenever feasible; as a
result, there's stuff on corporate welfare in pretty
much every issue. Earth Island can be reached at
300 Broadway #28, San Francisco CA 94133
• phone: 415 788 3666 • fax: 415 788 7324
• e-mail: earthisland@earthisland.org.

Too Much is a newsletter "devoted to capping
excessive income and wealth." It's published by
the Council on International and Public Affairs,
777 United Nations Plaza, #3C, New York NY
10017 • phone and fax: 800 316 2739 or 914
271 6500. Apex Press (same address and phone)
puts out a number of books, and distributes other
publishers' books as well.

Books

David Korten, ***When Corporations Rule the Earth***,
Kumarian Press, 1995. A very important book,
which tells how bad it's gotten, and offers clear-
headed solutions.

Alexander Cockburn and Ken Silverstein, ***Washington Babylon***, Verso, 1996. A withering look at the
corruption of both political parties, which sustains
the wealthfare system.

Randy Albelda, Nancy Folbre & the Center for Popular Economics, ***The War on the Poor: A Defense
Manual***, The New Press, 1996. A short, simple and
visually arresting look at the politics of poverty.

Carl Jensen and Project Censored, *Censored: The News That Didn't Make the News—and Why*, Seven Stories, 1996. Published annually, it regularly contains examples of welfare for the rich which—surprise!—don't make it into the mainstream media.

Charles Lewis and the Center for Public Integrity, *The Buying of the President*, Avon, 1996. Required reading for any voter, this book documents who owns whom in the 1996 presidential race.

Ralph Estes, *Who Pays? Who Profits? The Truth About the American Tax System*, IPS Books, 1993. A brief Q&A-style look at the gross unfairness of it all.

William Greider, *Who Will Tell the People*, Touchstone, 1993. Sadly recounts the extent to which private interests dominate public policy.

Paul Hawken, *The Ecology of Commerce: A Declaration of Sustainability*, HarperCollins, 1993. A possibly over-optimistic look at how we can prevent corporations from trashing the planet.

Russell Mokhiber, *Corporate Crime and Violence*, Sierra Club Books, 1989. A historical overview—not to be read before bedtime.

Kevin Phillips, *The Politics of Rich and Poor*, Random House, 1990. Phillips, an alleged Republican, surveys income disparity in the aftermath of the Reagan era.

Donald L. Barlett and James B. Steele, *America: Who Really Pays the Taxes*, Touchstone, 1994. Describes enough tax loopholes for the wealthy to enrage any hard-working wage earner.

GLOSSARY

amortization

When you amortize something, you spread the cost of it over time—either in reality or in your calculations. Say you're thinking of installing a solar water heating system. You might amortize the cost by dividing it by the monthly savings you expect to get on your utility bill. This would give you the number of months till payback—the point at which the system would begin saving you money. (To be accurate, you'd also have to figure in the interest you'd lose on the money you spent on the system, and which therefore couldn't be invested somewhere else.)

In mortgages, the cost of a house (or whatever), plus interest on the loan, are amortized into a series of monthly payments. *Depreciation* is another form of amortization.

averages

When you use the word *average* in everyday speech, you're usually talking about the *mean*—which you get by adding up all the numbers and dividing by how many numbers there are. But there are two other kinds of averages—the *median* and the *mode*—and they sometimes give a more accurate picture of what we're actually thinking of when we say "average."

Let's say we're doing a survey of incomes in Brunei (a little oil-producing enclave carved out of the island of Borneo by the British). To make things simple, let's say that Brunei only has eleven inhabitants: the sultan, who makes a billion dollars a year; two counselors to the sultan, who make $100,000 a year; three merchants, who make $10,000 a year; and five laborers, who make $1000 a year.

To get the *mean*, we add up everyone's annual income ($1,000,000,000 + $200,000 + $30,000 + $5,000) and divide by eleven; this comes to an annual income of about $91 million. But it's obviously very misleading to say that the average person in our hypothetical Brunei makes $91 million a year, since nobody makes anything like that amount—the sultan makes much more, and everybody else makes much less. That's where the median and the mode come in.

The *median* is the middle value in the distribution, the one halfway between the top and the bottom. Since there are eleven inhabitants, we're looking for the sixth income counting from either the top or the bottom, the one with five incomes above it and five below it. As you can see from the chart on the next page, this makes the median income $10,000.

In this case, the median obviously gives a much better idea of the average income than the mean does. (It does the same when we're talking about incomes in the US. If you use the mean instead of the median, huge incomes at the top skew it upwards and give a misleadingly optimistic picture of what the average American actually makes.)

The *mode* is the value that occurs the most frequently. In this distribution, it's $1,000, since five laborers make that amount and no more than three people make any other amount. The mode is the value you'd get most often if you picked inhabitants at random and asked them to tell you their incomes. (In fact, $1,000 is the answer you'd get 45% of the time.)

So, in this example, the mode also provides a much better idea of the average than the mean does. (The mode isn't typically at the bottom of the distribution, by the way; often it's near the median.)

Here's our example in chart form:

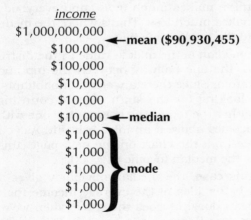

income

$1,000,000,000
$100,000 ◄— **mean ($90,930,455)**
$100,000
$10,000
$10,000
$10,000 ◄— **median**
$1,000
$1,000
$1,000 **} mode**
$1,000
$1,000

billion

Numbers in the billions contain three commas. A billion dollars is a thousand times more than a million dollars. It's equal to a stack of crisp, new dollar bills twelve times as high as the Empire State Building.

If you laid those dollar bills end-to-end, they'd stretch from New York to Los Angeles and back sixteen times, and you'd still have enough left over to go from New York to Mexico City and back.

Let's say you took a road trip. If you really pushed it, you might be able to drive an average of twelve hours a day (not counting gas stops, meals, sleep, etc.). If you drove seven days a week and averaged 65 while moving, it would take you almost four months to drive past a billion dollars' worth of dollar bills.

But a billion dollars is *nothing* compared to a trillion dollars.

black budgets

Both the Pentagon and the various intelligence agencies have secret "black budgets" that are completely off the books. Despite a Supreme Court ruling to the contrary, black budgets clearly violate the Constitution, which states that "no money shall be drawn from the Treasury, but in consequence of appropriations made by law" and requires that the government publish a "regular statement...of the receipts and expenditures of all public money."

Congressional Black Caucus

This policy-planning group consists of the African-American members of Congress.

constant dollars

Due to *inflation* (or, very rarely, *deflation*), the value of a dollar is always changing. So if you contrast how much something cost in, say,

1980 with how much it costs today, you're not going to get an accurate comparison. The way around that is to pick what the dollar was worth in a given year and make that the standard. Then you can say, "the project was expected to cost $2.3 billion in 1980, but ended up costing $7.8 billion (in 1980 dollars)."

credit — see *tax credit*

debt
The federal debt is the cumulative figure for how much the government owes at a given point in time (in other words, it's the total of all the *deficits,* minus any surpluses). In late 1996, the debt stood at slightly more than $5 trillion.

deduction — see *tax deduction*

deficit
The federal budget deficit is how much expenditures exceed revenues in a given fiscal year. In fiscal 1995, it was $164 billion, and it's projected at $117 billion for fiscal 1996. Compare *debt.*

deflation
Deflation is when, over time, a given amount of money is able to buy more and more things. Compare *inflation.*

depreciation
Depreciation allows you to deduct a certain part of the cost of an asset from your taxable income each year, supposedly to allow for the decrease in its value as it ages. (Thus it's a kind of *amortization.) Depreciation schedules*

tell you how much you can take off each year; they vary with the type of property, and with changes in the tax code.

depression
A depression is simply a really bad *recession*. (There isn't a generally agreed upon benchmark for when a recession becomes a depression, but some people say it's when unemployment reaches 20%.)

family — see *household*

federal debt or deficit — see *debt* or *deficit*

fiscal year
A fiscal year is any twelve-month period an organization (a corporation, governmental entity or whatever) uses for its budgets. It can be the same as a calendar year (January 1 to December 31) but often isn't.

The federal government's fiscal years begin on October 1st and are named after the calendar year in which they end. So fiscal year 1996—typically abbreviated *FY96*—began October 1, 1995 and ended September 30, 1996.

GDP — see *gross domestic product*

general fund revenues
These include all federal revenues except for entitlement programs like Social Security and Medicare, which aren't discretionary and which are provided for by separate trust funds (at least they *were* separate, before greedy politicians got their hands on them). Combining entitlements with general fund

revenues is a trick politicians play to hide how much money they're spending on discretionary items like the military budget.

GNP — see *gross national product*

gross domestic product

The gross domestic product (or *GDP*) is the total market value of the goods and services brought into final use in a nation in a certain period of time (usually a year). It became the official measure of the US economy in 1991, replacing the *gross national product*.

This change brought us into line with the way most other industrialized nations figure it, thus making comparisons easier. (For the US, the GDP and the GNP are very similar.)

gross national product

The gross national product (or *GNP*) is the *gross domestic product* plus income earned by the nation's residents in foreign investments, minus income earned by foreign investors in the domestic market. In other words, the GNP measures what's produced by a nation's citizens, regardless of where they're located.

household

The Census Bureau distinguishes between a *household* (any group of people living together) and a *family* (an "economic unit" joined by marriage). That's why figures for median household income (or net worth) are different from those for family income (or net worth).

House Progressive Caucus
This policy-planning group consists of progressive members of the House of Representatives.

income disparity
As its name implies, this measures how evenly or unevenly income is distributed among people in a particular group (usually a nation). Of course, there can be different kinds of income disparity. In Saudi Arabia, for example, few people are really poor and a relatively small group make *tons* of money.

In the United States, many more people are poor and many more are rich (although few make as much as the richest Saudis). These varieties of income distribution complicate the question of how to measure income disparity, but if you just want to know if a nation has a lot of income disparity or a little, it usually isn't hard to tell.

inflation
Inflation is when, over time, a given amount of money is able to buy fewer and fewer things. Compare *deflation*.

mean — see *averages*

means testing
Means testing is figuring out how much money someone has, in order to decide if they're eligible for a welfare program that's only supposed to be open to people with low incomes and few assets.

median — see *averages*

million

Numbers in the millions contain two commas. A million dollars is a thousand times more than a thousand dollars. Laid end-to-end, a million dollars' worth of dollar bills would stretch almost 95 miles.

Imagine yourself driving by them. You're doing 65, so they're just a blur there by the side of the road. Still, it takes you almost an hour and a half to get past all those bills.

But a million dollars is nothing compared to a billion dollars.

mode — see *averages*

multinational — see *transnational*

PAC

A PAC (the name is short for *political action committee*) is basically just a way to get around limits on campaign contributions. Also, by bundling many small-to-medium-sized donations, PACs have more influence. A politician may not know—or care—what industry you're associated with if you send in a $100 donation, but that's never the case when $5000 or $10,000 comes from a PAC.

perk

A perk—short for *perquisite*—is an extra benefit, beyond salary, that someone gets by virtue of being in a certain job (or unpaid position). For example, a company pays for a business flight but the employee who makes the flight gets the frequent flyer miles. (*Fringe benefit* means almost the same thing as *perk*, but a perk is much more likely to be an unofficial benefit that isn't explicitly stated anywhere.)

prime rate
Theoretically, the prime rate is the lowest interest a bank charges (on money it lends to its best customers). More typically, it's an arbitrary benchmark to which other interest rates are pegged.

progressive tax
With a progressive tax, the more money you make, the higher the percentage of it you pay in taxes. US income tax is supposed to be progressive. Compare *regressive tax*.

recession
A recession is usually defined as a decline in general business activity (as measured by the *GDP*) that goes on for at least two or three quarters (that is, for six to nine months). When a recession is really bad, it's called a *depression*.

regressive tax
With a regressive tax, the less money you make, the higher the percentage of it you pay in taxes. Many new tax proposals—as well as many existing provisions—are in fact regressive (the Social Security tax is a good example). Compare *progressive tax*.

revenues
Money coming in to the government. Also see *general fund revenues*.

tax credit

A tax credit lets you subtract an expense from the taxes you owe, not merely from your income (as a *tax deduction* does). Depending on your tax bracket, a credit is currently worth about $2\frac{1}{2}$ to 7 times more than a deduction of the same size.

tax deduction

A tax deduction lets you subtract an expense from the income you report on your tax return. Compare *tax credit*.

transnational

A transnational—or *multinational*—is simply a corporation that has operations in more than one country. Typically, however, the term is used to refer to the larger transnationals, which are richer than many countries and more powerful than most. (We prefer the term *transnationals* to *multinationals* because it's better at giving the flavor of how they soar over and subsume mere nations.)

trillion

Numbers in the trillions contain four commas. A trillion dollars is a thousand times more than a billion dollars and a million times more than a million dollars.

A trillion dollars is equal to a stack of crisp, new dollar bills almost three thousand miles high. If you laid that pile down on its side, packed tightly together, it would stretch from New York to Los Angeles.

If you took that same trillion dollars in dollar bills and laid it down end-to-end, it would stretch from New York to Los Angeles and back about *17,000 times*—or from the earth to the sun and then around it.

If you started a business the day Christ was born and it lost a million dollars *a day*, you'd still have more than 700 years to go before you lost a trillion dollars.

WELFARE FOR THE POOR

Federal expenditures on welfare for the poor cost around $130 billion in fiscal year 1996. There are two basic categories of benefits—those that go exclusively to the poor (or are supposed to) and those that go partially to the poor. The following programs fall into the first group:

- ***Food stamps***—$26 billion. (This program was severely cut back by the 1996 welfare "reform" bill.)

- ***AFDC*** (Aid to Families with Dependent Children)—$18 billion. Along with food stamps, AFDC is what most people think of as "welfare." It's always been controversial because it's mostly geared towards women who are raising children without male support. (AFDC was essentially abolished by the 1996 welfare "reform" bill.)

- ***Housing assistance***—$13.1 billion. Section 8 helps families living in private housing keep their rent below 30% of their family income (at a cost of $9.8 billion a year); a similar program does the same thing for people living in public housing projects ($3.3 billion a year). Between them, they cost about half of the $26 billion in wealthfare rich homeowners receive (as described in that chapter).

- **WIC** (Women, Infants and Children Food and Nutrition Information Program)—$8.2 billion. WIC provides poor women and children with vouchers for nutritional counseling, referrals to other programs and some food items. WIC isn't an entitlement program—it's offered only if funds are available. Many states have waiting lists of people who want to get on WIC.

- **Head Start**—$3.6 billion. Since 1965, Head Start has provided preschool readiness programs, and health and nutrition services, to children whose families live below the poverty line. Regarded as one of the most successful federal programs, Head Start has never been funded well enough to serve everyone who qualifies for it.

- **Low-income energy assistance**—$1.3 billion. This program provides funds for heating, cooling and other weather-related and emergency needs for families at or below 110% of the poverty line. (Some states provide funding beyond the federal government's.)

- **JOBS** (Job Opportunities and Basic Skills) program—$1 billion. This program provides education, training and employment placements to AFDC recipients. It requires mothers with children as young as three to get into the workforce or lose their AFDC benefits.

- **Legal Services Corporation**—$280 million. Legal Services helps poor people deal with civil—not criminal—matters like divorces, consumer fraud, housing, jobs, education and entitlement benefits.

These programs total about $71.5 billion, and we count that entire amount as welfare for the poor. For five other programs, things are more complicated.

The largest of thes[...]
$82 billion in fisc[...]
Medicare, because [...]
for the elderly regar[...]

Medicaid pays me[...]
and for blind, dis[...]
whose medical cost[...]
matter what that [...]
homes now costin[...]
you don't have to be poor not to be able to
afford medical care.)

In theory, you're not eligible for Medicaid if
you have more than $4,000 in assets, but
your house doesn't count, nor do your
spouse's assets or income. You can even
transfer up to $70,000 of your assets to your
spouse, as well as $1800 a month ($21,600 a
year) of your own income. These loopholes led
Consumers' Research magazine to call Medicaid "one of the largest middle-class entitlement programs on the books."

Even millionaires can receive Medicaid benefits, simply by transferring assets to their
children three years before applying (although
this could cost a lot in gift taxes). An entire
industry has sprung up, running seminars
that teach people how to mine Medicaid.

While 73% of Medicaid recipients are on
AFDC, they receive only 31% of the total benefits. The other 69% of the money goes to
people who may or may not be poor; all we
know about them for sure is that their medical bills run, on average, six times higher
than AFDC recipients'.

lot of Medicaid money goes to
cal companies, makers of medical
, hospital owners, doctors and oth-
ny people who are famous for over-
ng for their products and services (and
's not even considering Medicaid fraud).
o even when Medicaid recipients are actually
poor, a large part of the program's funding
ends up going to wealthy price-gougers.

Then there's **SSI** (Supplemental Security
Income), which came to $18 billion in fiscal
1996. SSI is supposed to provide a guaran-
teed income to blind, disabled or elderly people with limited assets and low incomes, but
the means testing is similar to that under
Medicaid. (Your spouse's income does count,
but not unearned income; your house doesn't
count, regardless of what it's worth.)

Pell grants are a federally funded scholar-
ship program that cost $6.3 billion in fiscal
1996. These funds are available to students
whose families make $30,000 a year or less
and have a net worth of up to $85,000. This
doesn't make them well-to-do, but since the
median net worth of US households is
$37,587—or was, in 1993—even households
that are quite a bit richer than average quali-
fy for Pell grants.

The ***earned income tax credit*** *(EITC)* is a
$5.7-billion tax break that applies only to the
working poor who make enough money to pay
taxes. As such, it's also wealthfare, because it
allows some companies to get away with paying their employees less than a living wage

(since the EITC supplements that wage). And it does nothing for the really poor.

Finally, there's the **school lunch and breakfast program**, which ran to $4.3 billion in fiscal 1996. Started in 1946, it serves about half of all school-aged children; in 1993, 48% of the households participating were below the poverty line.

(15% of all Americans—22% of all children, 46% of all black children—live at or below the poverty line, which is currently set at an annual income of $12,590 for a family of three, $15,150 for a family of four. 45% of these people get Medicaid, 35% food stamps, 29% school lunches and breakfasts, and 21% public housing.)

So—how are we going to figure out what portion of Medicaid, SSI, Pell grants, EITC and school lunches should count as welfare for the poor? There isn't a clear answer for any of these programs, and of course there's also the question of where to draw the line for what we call "poor."

If the focus of this book were welfare for the poor, rather than welfare for the rich, we'd have analyzed this issue more thoroughly, but since it isn't, our best estimate is that half the money spent on this second category of programs should be counted.

If that seems too low to you, feel free to pick another percentage. But one thing is clear: 100% is too high. There's no way these programs serve the poor exclusively.

These five programs cost a total of about $116 billion a year, and half of that is $58 billion. Add the $71.5 billion spent on programs that serve the poor exclusively, and you get $129.5 billion as a total for welfare for the poor (let's call it an even $130 billion).

Of course, all these figures represent funding levels *before* the welfare "reform" bill of 1996, and will be much lower in the immediate future.

WHERE WE GOT OUR FACTS

*Chapter titles are **bold italic**. Page numbers are **boldface**. Sections within chapters (when indicated) are <u>italic underline</u>.*

Rather than use op. cit. and ibid, we just repeat the (first) author's name. When we're referring to an earlier work than the last one mentioned, we repeat the title as well.

Introduction

6. *Federal deficit. Arizona Daily Star*, 7/23/96, p. 3.

Federal budget. War Resisters League, "Where Your Income Tax Money Really Goes," *Z Magazine,* 5/96, p. 66.

Federal debt. Arizona Daily Star, 7/23/96.

8. *Head Start.* Lois Stevens, "Speaking Out for Head Start," *Entry Point: The Quarterly Newsletter of RESULTS,* Summer 1996, p. 1.

9. *Conflicting subsidies.* See the agribusiness chapter.

10. *Corporate tax rates.* Donald L. Barlett and James B. Steele, *America: Who Really Pays the Taxes,* Touchstone, 1994, p. 140. (The 11% figure is an update—per Janice Shields, in conversation. The number in Barlett & Steele is 15%.)

Series of tax "reforms." William Greider, *Who Will Tell the People*, Touchstone, 1992, p. 80.

10–11. *1983–89 wealth increase.* Edward N. Wolff, "Time for a Wealth Tax?" *Boston Review,* 2–3/96.

11. *Net worth of top 1%.* Chuck Collins, *Tax Day '96 Organizing Kit,* Share the Wealth, 1996.

Wealth within top 20%. Paul Krugman, "What the Public Doesn't Know Can't Hurt Us," *Washington Monthly,* 10/95, pp. 8–12.

400 wealthiest families. Kevin Phillips, *The Politics of Rich and Poor,* Random House, 1990, p. 166.

Military waste and fraud

13–14. *Fiscal 1996 Pentagon budget.* Anthony Lewis, "The Defense Anomaly," *New York Times,* 1/22/96, p. A15.

$7 billion more than requested. "Bunker Bill," *The Nation,* 12/25/95, p. 812.

14. *5% of GNP.* Linda Rothstein, Lauren Spain and Danielle Gordon, "A Sense of Proportion," *Bulletin of the Atomic Scientists,* 9–10/95, pp. 32–33.

Military budgets of great powers. "Last of the Big Time Spenders," Center for Defense Information, *Defense Monitor,* 4–5/96.

Compared to "regional adversaries." Rothstein.

37% of world military spending. Lewis.

22% of world economy. World Military Expenditures and Arms Transfers, US Government Printing Office, 2/95.

14–15. *CDI estimates. Defense Monitor,* 4–5/96.

WRL estimates. War Resisters League.

<u>Waste beyond your wildest dreams</u>

15. *$13 billion lost; $15 billion unaccounted for.* Colman McCarthy, "Military has real money, fake enemy," *National Catholic Reporter,* 6/30/95, p. 20.

Anthony Lewis quote. Lewis.

15–16. *Colman McCarthy quote.* McCarthy.

16. *Navy purchase orders, etc.* Colleen O'Connor, "The Waste Goes On—And On and On," *The Nation,* 10/4/93, pp. 350–51.

16–17. *Overpriced supplies.* Christopher Cerf and Henry Beard, *The Pentagon Catalog,* Workman, 1986.

17. *What the Pentagon usually pays.* "Going commercial," *The Economist,* 9/3/94, special section, p. 13.

17–18. *VA examples.* Michael Isikoff, "Out of the Line of Fire," *Newsweek,* 3/20/95, pp. 28–29.

Career criminals

18. *Every one of top ten weapons contractors.* Rothstein.

18–19. *Grumman, Lockheed, Northrop and Rockwell examples.* J. Whitfield Larrabee, "Black Holes," *The Humanist,* 5–6/96, pp. 13–14.

19. *85 instances.* Project on Government Oversight (PGO), *Survey of Defense Contractor Signatories,* 1995.

Boeing, Grumman, Hughes, Raytheon and RCA. Department of Defense Inspector General (DOD IG), *Semiannual Report to the Congress,* 10/1/89–3/31/90, pp. 3–8.

Hughes procurement fraud. General Accounting Office (GAO), *Defense Procurement Fraud,* 9/92.

Teledyne false testing. DOD IG, 4/1–9/30/90, pp. 3–13.

McDonnell Douglas "defective pricing." GAO and PGO.

GE procurement and mail fraud. GAO.

1961 GE case. Russell Mokhiber, *Corporate Crime and Violence,* Sierra Club Books, 1989, p. 219.

19–20. *1977 to first 1985 case.* Greider, pp. 350–52.

20. *Second 1985 case.* Andy Pasztor, *When the Pentagon Was for Sale,* Scribner, 1995, p. 31.

1989 and 1990 cases. Greider.

GE sells weapons division. John Holusha, "Delay in Martin Marietta's Purchase of GE Unit," *New York Times,* 1/23/93, p. 39.

20–21. *Operation Ill Wind.* Pasztor, pp. 37–38.

21. *70 out of 100 suppliers.* Pasztor, p. 366.

Weapons industry's net income. Howard Banks, "Aerospace and Defense," *Forbes,* 1/2/95, pp. 126–27 and 1/1/96, pp. 80–81.

The black budget

22. *CIA's share.* John Pike, Federation of American Scientists, telephone interview, 6/96.

Debate in Congress. Bob Benenson, "Budget Secrecy Openly Debated," *Congressional Quarterly Weekly Report,* 7/23/94, p. 2061.

Pike estimates. Pike, telephone interview, 6/96.

B-2 cost projection. Larrabee, p. 11.

23. *MILSTAR.* Tim Weiner, *Blank Check: The Pentagon's Black Budget,* Warner Books, 1990, pp. 46–47.

Pentagon employee quote. Larrabee, p. 10.

Quotes from Constitution. Article 1, Section 9, Clause 7.

Don't call it bribery

23–24. *Defense PACs.* Alexander Cockburn and Ken Silverstein, *Washington Babylon*, Verso, 1996, p. 164.

24. *Spending in congressional districts.* Rothstein.

Dicks and Stevens. Larrabee.

B-2 spending. Larrabee.

24–25. *Maxine Waters.* William D. Hartung, "An Indefensible Budget," *Harper's*, 11/95, p. 27.

25. *Seawolf not needed.* Lauren Spain, "Chasing the phantom fleet," *Bulletin of the Atomic Scientists*, 9–10/95, p. 45.

Liberal Senators' support. John Isaacs, "Not in my District," *Bulletin of the Atomic Scientists*, 9–10/94, pp. 13–15.

V-22 unwanted. Robert L. Borosage, "All dollars, no sense," *Mother Jones*, 9–10/93, p. 41.

What about the jobs we'd lose?

Two jobs for one. Roanoke Times, 1/25/93, p. A7.

CBO estimates. "Why We Overfeed the Sacred Cow," *Defense Monitor*, 2/96.

26. *Eisenhower quote.* Mike Moore, "More security, less money," *Bulletin of the Atomic Scientists*, 9–10/95, p. 37.

800,000 jobs gone. Moore, p. 36.

Layoffs in nonmilitary divisions. Danielle Gordon, "Prosperity for whom?," *Bulletin of the Atomic Scientists*, 9–10/95, p. 43.

Drop in Pentagon budgets. Alexander Cockburn, "Beat the Devil," *The Nation*, 12/11/95, p. 736.

Eight companies' layoffs. Gordon.

The revolving door

27. *Weinberger and Shultz.* James McCartney, *Friends in High Places*, Ballantine, 1989, pp. 169–74.

Paisley & Lehman, Pasztor, pp. 74, 96.

Perry & Deutch, William D. Hartung, "Stormin' Norman," *Washington Post*, 7/28/96, p. C1.

Lavish entertaining of contractors. Pasztor, p. 36.

Direct handouts

27–28. *Lockheed Martin bonuses.* William D. Hartung, "Welfare Kings," *The Nation*, 6/19/95, p. 873–74.

28. *State Dep't foreign aid.* Eyal Press, "Prez Pampers Peddlers of Pain," *The Nation*, 10/3/94, p. 340.

28–29. *General Dynamics and Lockheed.* Ralph Nader, "Washington's Holiday Gift Exchange," press release, 12/25/95.

29. *$5.4 billion a year.* Janice Shields, *Aid for Dependent Corporations (AFDC) 1995*, Essential Information,1995.

43% of world weapons trade. *Arizona Daily Star*, 6/14/96, p. 10.

Egyptian debt forgiven. Ramsey Clark, *The Fire This Time*, Thunder's Mouth Press, 1993, p. 155.

Selling the story to the public

Vandenberg quote. Benjamin Schwarz, "Why America Thinks It Has to Rule the World," *Atlantic Monthly*, 6/96, p. 94.

29–30. *Soviet "threat."* Tom Gervasi, *The Myth of Soviet Military Superiority*, Harper & Row, 1986.

30. *Seven other "gaps."* Sherwood Ross, "The Progressive Interview: Seymour Melman," *The Progressive*, 2/92, pp. 34–36.

Star Wars scam. Lauren Spain, "The dream of missile defense," *Bulletin of the Atomic Scientists*, 9–10/95, pp. 49–50.

Star Wars bullet quote. John Pike, Federation of American Scientists, telephone interview, 6/96.

Faked Star Wars tests. Tim Weiner, "Lies and Rigged 'Star Wars' Tests Fooled the Kremlin—and Congress," *New York Times*, 8/18/93, p. 1.

30–31. *$35 billion.* Spain.

31. *Clinton weasel-fest.* Spain.

Pentagon budget levels. Lauren Spain, "The competition has bowed out," *Bulletin of the Atomic Scientists*, 9–10/95, p. 39.

32. *Two-war plan.* Editors, "One, Two, Many Wars," *The Progressive*, 10/93, pp. 9–10.

How much military spending is waste?

Trident missles. Danielle Gordon, "More missiles, fewer targets," *Bulletin of the Atomic Scientists*, 9–10/95, p. 47.

C-5s and C-144s. Lauren Spain, "The C-17: A $340 million ugly duckling," *Bulletin of the Atomic Scientists*, 9–10/95, pp. 46–47.

32–33. *F-22 fighter.* Lauren Spain, "A stealthy $72 billion," *Bulletin of the Atomic Scientists*, 9–10/95, p. 46.

33. *Duplication between services.* John Isaacs, "Pentagon clings to costly lifestyle," *Bulletin of the Atomic Scientists*, 4/93, p. 3.

Troops abroad. Borosage.

$3.5-billion aircraft carrier. O'Connor.

34. *Korb estimate.* Borosage.

Atomic Scientists' estimate. Jerome Wiesner, Philip Morrison and Kosta Tsipis, "Ending Overkill," *Bulletin of the Atomic Scientists,* 3/93, pp. 12–23.

CDI estimate. "The 1997 Military Budget: A Ticking Time Bomb," *Defense Monitor,* 4–5/96.

Social Security tax inequities

35. *Reagan quote.* Ronnie Dugger, *Reagan: The Man and His Presidency,* McGraw Hill, 1983, p. 111.

Largest tax increase. Greider, p. 92.

35–36. *SS tax up, other taxes down.* Greider.

36. *SS tax as percentage of income.* Barlett, p. 104.

Change in combined tax bills. Barbara Ehrenreich, "Helping the Rich Stay That Way," *Time,* 4/18/94, p. 86.

37. *Trust fund shortfalls.* Harry Figgie, Jr., and Gerald Swanson, *Bankruptcy 1995: The Coming Collapse of America and How to Stop It* (3rd ed.), Little, Brown, 1993, p. 57.

Unified budget. Barlett, p. 100.

38. *SS receipts and outlays.* Figgie, p. 72.

Additional $53 billion. Robert McIntyre, Citizens for Tax Justice, telephone interview, 7/96.

Accelerated depreciation

Nixon executive order. Robert McIntyre, *Tax Expenditures—The Hidden Entitlements,* Citizens for Tax Justice, 1996, p. 11.

1981 tax plan. Robert J. Shapiro, *Paying for Progress,* Progressive Policy Institute, 2/91.

38–39. *250 largest companies.* McIntyre, p. 12.

39. *1986 tax reform.* McIntyre.

38–39. *$37 billion cost.* McIntyre, p. 55.

Trading leases and tax credits. McIntyre, p. 13.

Reagan Treasury offical quote. McIntyre.

39–40. *Effect on economy.* McIntyre, p. 12.

40. *Westinghouse and American Brands examples.* Ralph Nader, "Take US Job Exporters Off Corporate Welfare," press release, 9/4/95.

Nader letter to CEOs. Ralph Nader, "CEOs Demand Balanced Budget But Won't Give Up Corporate Welfare," press release, 6/7/96.

41. *Tax breaks by income.* McIntyre, p. 13.

Lower taxes on capital gains

41. *8% to incomes below $50,000.* McIntyre, p. 15.

Other statistics in that ¶. Barlett, p. 30.

41–42. *97% to richest 1%.* McIntyre, p. 19.

42. *Armey and Forbes flat tax.* McIntyre, p. 21.

History of capital gains rates. Citizens for Tax Justice, "Top Federal Tax Rates Since 1916," press release, 6/96.

Timber and mining tax breaks. Courtney Cuff, Ralph De Gennaro and Gawain Kripke, *Green Scissors Report*, Friends of the Earth, 1/96.

43. *Certain small business stocks.* McIntyre, p. 20.

Starker exchanges. McIntyre.

Death and gift exemptions. McIntyre.

44. *Capital gains, employment and growth.* McIntyre, p. 18.

$37 billion cost. McIntyre, p. 55.

The S&L bailout

45. *History of thrifts.* Robert Sherrill, "The Looting Decade: S&Ls, Big Banks and Other Triumphs of Capitalism," *The Nation*, 11/19/90, pp. 592–93.

Volcker and Greenspan ignored unemployment. Robert Sherrill, "The Inflation of Alan Greenspan," *The Nation*, 3/11/96, pp. 11–15. William Greider, *Secrets of the Temple*, Simon & Schuster, 1987.

45–46. *Inflation, prime rate, unemployment. Statistical Abstract of the United States*, US Government Printing Office, 1995.

46. *Volcker and Sherrill quotes.* Robert Sherrill, "The Looting Decade: S&Ls, Big Banks and Other Triumphs of Capitalism," *The Nation*, 11/19/90, p. 592.

46–47. *Situation in 1981.* Sherrill, p. 593.

47. *St Germain in 1980.* Brooks Jackson, *Honest Graft*, Knopf, 1988, p. 203.

St Germain in 1982. Sherrill, pp. 594–95.

Reagan administration's actions. Stephen Pizzo, Mary Fricker and Paul Muolo, *Inside Job: The Looting of America's Savings and Loans*, Harper Perennial, 1991, p. 26.

48. *Oldenberg, Beebe and Dixon.* Pizzo, pp. 236–37, 251–55, 436.

Silverado and prospective borrower. Sherrill, p. 609.

Silverado delay cost a billion. Sherrill, p. 610.

49. *CIA connection.* Pete Brewton, *The Mafia, The CIA & George Bush*, SPI Books, 1992.

A billion dollars a month. Sherrill, p. 609.

Dukakis tried to raise issue. Sherrill, p. 608.

Bentsen part-owner of S&Ls. Brewton, p. 4.

49–50. *Growing bailout costs.* Sherrill, p. 593.

50. *Bass and Perelman.* Sherrill, pp. 610–11.

51. *Bailout costs.* Sherrill, p. 620.

Average sentences. Sherrill, p. 618.

52. *Authors of* Inside Job. Pizzo, p. 20.

Homeowners' tax breaks

52. *Beginning statistics.* Vicki Kemper, "Home Inequities," *Common Cause Magazine*, Summer 1994, p. 14.

Home ownership in Canada. Peter G. Peterson, *Facing Up*, Simon & Schuster, 1993, p. 110.

52–53. *Deductions vs. income levels.* McIntyre, p. 43.

53. *NHI calculations.* Peter Dreier, "The GOP's Cynical Attack on Public Housing," National Housing Institute, 1996.

PPI calculations. Robert J. Shapiro, *Cut-and-Invest: A Budget Strategy for the New Economy*, Progressive Policy Institute, 3/95.

CBC calculations. Joel Bleifuss, "The First Stone," *In These Times*, 11/13/95.

Packwood's proposal. Dreier.

54. *Concord Coalition proposal. The Zero Deficit Plan*, The Concord Coalition, 5/95.

55/$125,000 exemption. Kemper.

White House estimates. Fiscal Year 1997 Budget of the United States, US Government Printing Office, 1996.

Trading up and deducting local taxes. Kemper.

55. *Home equity deductions.* Kemper.

Phasing out deduction. Shapiro.

Agribusiness subsidies

56. *Average farmer's worth.* Richard J. Dennis, "Privilege & Poverty," *Reason*, 4/93, p. 29.

Who gets the subsidies? C. Ford Runge, John Schnittker and Timothy Penny, *Ending Agricultural Entitlements: How to Fix Farm Policy*, Progressive Foundation, 5/95.

57. *Who's a farmer? City Slickers,* Environmental Working Group, 3/95.

The "cheaper food" ruse

58. *Sugar prices.* Jim Phillips, "Who Gets What from USDA," *Progressive Farmer,* 10/95.

Dairy and peanut prices. Alan Rosenfeld, Public Voice, telephone interview, 7/96.

Livestock subsidies

Livestock tax breaks. Dawn Erlandson, Jessica Few and Gawain Kripke, *Dirty Little Secrets,* Friends of the Earth, 4/95.

59. *Quarter of market value.* Carl Deal, *The Greenpeace Guide to Anti-environmental Organizations,* Odonian Press, 1993, p. 82.

BLM grazing "economics." Edward A. Chadd, "Manifest Subsidy," *Common Cause Magazine,* Fall 1995, pp. 18–21.

Subsidies for drug peddlers

Tobacco death toll. American Cancer Society, Tobacco Use, http://www.cancer.org/tobacco.html

Durbin proposal. David Hosansky, "Under Fire From All Sides, Tobacco Program Thrives," *Congressional Quarterly Weekly Report,* 12/2/95, p. 3648.

Higher consumer costs. Joseph Califano, "In reply," *Journal of the AMA,* 3/22–29/95, p. 919.

60. *Tobacco PACs.* Ed Mierzwinski, "Tobacco PAC Contributions to Congress," Public Interest Research Group press release, 3/14/96.

Tobacco export pressure. American Cancer Society.

Effects on South Korea. Editors, "Tobacco Imperialism," *Multinational Monitor,* 1–2/92.

Deficiency payments

61. *Deficiency payment details.* Environmental Working Group, "Summary Analysis of USDA Subsidy Payments, 1985–1994," press release, 7/96.

61–62. *1996 farm bill.* Kenneth Cook, *Freedom to Farm,* Environmental Working Group, 2/27/96.

The waters of Babylon

63. *Getting around the 960-acre limit.* Cuff.

Construction costs. Chadd.

Lost interest on construction costs. Cuff.

Cost of water subsidies. Chadd.

California corporate farmers. San Francisco Chronicle, 1/29/89.

64. Subsidized water resold to local government. Chadd.

Miscellaneous pork

Stephen Moore and Dean Stansel, How Corporate Welfare Won, Cato Institute, 5/15/96.

The welfare king

65. 43% of ADM profits. James Bovard, Archer Daniels Midland: A Case Study in Corporate Welfare, Cato Institute, 9/26/95.

$100,000 to Nixon. Dan Carney, "Dwayne's World," Mother Jones, 7–8/95, p. 44.

$25,000 to Barker. Bovard.

Contributions to Clinton and Dole. Charles Lewis, The Buying of the President, Avon, 1996, p. 10.

$100,000 to Dole Foundation. Bovard.

Apartment. Carney.

Free trips and Red Cross donation. Bovard.

$1.4 million in contributions. Carney.

"Tithing." Bovard.

The ethanol handout

66. Ethanol vs. gasoline. Bovard.

67. 5.4¢ tax credit. Carney.

Cost of ethanol vs. gasoline. Bovard.

Size of subsidy. FY97 Budget.

ADM's share. Carney.

How sweet it is.

68. Clinton, Dole and Andreas. Carney.

Tax avoidance by transnationals

69. "Why man, he doth bestride..." William Shakespeare, Julius Caesar, act I, scene 2, lines 135–38.

69–70. Transfer pricing. McIntyre, p. 23.

70–71. How much tax transnationals paid. Barlett, p. 190.

71–72. Puerto Rican tax exemptions. McIntyre, p. 24.

72. Credit for foreign taxes. McIntyre, pp. 22–24.

Saudi corporate income tax. Barlett, pp. 183–89.

72–73. Intel's "nowhere income." McIntyre, p. 23.

73. *Incentive to ship jobs abroad.* Ralph Estes, *Who Pays? Who Profits? The Truth About the American Tax System,* IPS Books, 1993, p. 40.

Cost estimate. McIntyre, p. 56.

Tax-free muni bonds
73–75. McIntyre, pp. 25–27.

Media handouts
75. *Network profits.* "Rhetoric and Reality," Campaign for Broadcast Competition, http://campaign.com/issue.html

75–76. *Cost of NY station.* Editorial, "GOP Giveaway," *Wall Street Journal,* 9/1/95, p. A26.

76–77. *Shifting to HDTV. Wall Street Journal.*

77. *Pro-giveaway commercials.* Arthur E. Rowse, "Off the Spectrum," *Extra!,* 7–8/96, pp. 16–17.

77. *Spectra—auctions and estimated value. Wall Street Journal.*

78. *Disney and Westinghouse stations; twelve stations in Texas.* Maria Mallory and Warren Cohen, "A league of their own," *US News and World Report,* 10/9/95, pp. 62–65.

Two stations in Norfolk. Baltimore Business Journal, 5/24/96.

Five suburban stations. Fairfield County Business Journal, 3/11/96.

79. *Corporate advertising total.* Mark Crispin Miller, "Free the Media," *The Nation,* 6/3/96, p. 12.

79–80. *80% proposal.* Steven W. Colford, "Clintonites eye ad deductibility," *Advertising Age,* 1/31/94, p. 4.

Excessive government pensions
80–82. Gareth G. Cook, "The Pension Time Bomb," *Washington Monthly,* 1–2/95, pp. 17–20.

Insurance loopholes
82–84. *Wal-Mart COLI.* Allan Sloan, "Deal of a Lifetime," *Newsweek,* 10/23/95, pp. 46–47.

84. *Originally for small businesses.* Lee A. Sheppard, "'Janitor' Insurance as a Tax Shelter," *Tax Notes,* 9/25/95.

84–85. *Other insurance loopholes.* McIntyre, p. 33–34.

Nuclear subsidies

85. *1948–95 figure.* Cuff.

1996 figure. Auke Piersma, Public Citizen, telephone interview, 6/96.

85–86. *Insurance subsidy.* Ted Weiss, "Ending the Unfair Underwriting of Nuclear Power," *USA Today Magazine,* 3/80, pp. 14–16.

86. *Chernobyl's total cost.* "The Nuclear Power Industry is at a Standstill," *USA Today Magazine,* 5/93, pp. 66–67.

Estimated cost of insurance subsidy. Energy Information Administration, "Federal Energy Subsidies," press release, 12/11/95.

86–87. *USEC.* Cuff.

87. *Argonne and Idaho.* Erlandson.

88–89. *Savannah River site and Yucca Mountain.* Cuff.

89. *PIRG quote.* Anna Aurelio, Public Interest Research Group, telephone interview, 6/96.

89–91. *Closing reactors down.* Sasha Abramsky, "Bracing for a Nuclear Bailout," *The Nation,* 9/25/95, pp. 312–14.

91–92. *Fusion research.* Cuff.

92–93. *"Next generation."* Cuff.

Aviation subsidies

94. *Boeing vs. Airbus.* Bruce Bernard, "EU suspects US of violating bilateral aircraft subsidy accord," *Journal of Commerce and Commercial,* 3/18/93.

95. *Government aviation subsidies.* Bernard.

CBC-suggested cuts. Congressional Black Caucus, "The FY 1996 CBC Alternative Budget: A Budget for the Caring Majority." 1995.

$4.5-billion estimate. Delaware Valley Association of Rail Passengers Newsletter, 2/96.

Business meals and entertainment

95–96. McIntyre.

Mining subsidies

96–97. *Babbitt press conference.* Jim Lyon, "Patenting Plunder Continues," press release, Mineral Policy Center, 9/26/95.

97. *Law of 1872.* Cuff.

American Barrick. Dan Hirschmann, "The Last American Dinosaur: The 1872 Mining Law," press release, Mineral Policy Center, 10/17/95.

Chevron and Manville. Cuff.

Total value of minerals extracted. Hirschmann.

98. *$300 million a year.* Shapiro.

Minerals left. Hirschmann.

98–100. *Other breaks for mining companies.* Erlandson.

Oil and gas tax breaks
100–103. Erlandson.

Export subsidies
103. *USDA subsidies.* Nader, "Washington's Holiday Gift Exchange."

Friends of the Earth point. Cuff.

104. *Cargill, Continental Grain, Louis Dreyfuss, Bunge, Ferruzzi, Pillsbury, Mitsubishi.* Janice Shields, "Aid for Foreign and US Corporations," Center for Study of Responsive Law, 1995.

Sunkist, McDonald's, Dole and American Legend. Stephen Moore and Dean Stansel, *Ending Corporate Welfare as We Know It*, Cato Institute, 1995.

Gallo, Campbell's, M&M/Mars. Moore and Stansel, *How Corporate Welfare Won.*

Miller Beer, General Mills. Cuff.

104–105. *Export-Import Bank.* William Greider, "The Ex-Im Files," *Rolling Stone*, 8/8/96, p. 51; Nader.

105. *OPIC.* Moore and Stansel; Nader, "Washington's Holiday Gift Exchange"and "Take US Job Exporters Off Corporate Welfare."

State Department subsidies. FY97 Budget.

Synfuel tax credits
106–107. Erlandson.

Timber subsidies
107. *Champion road-builder.* Cuff.

107–108. *Trading trees for roads.* Randall O'Toole, Thoreau Institute, telephone interview, 6/96.

108. *Value of $2.85.* Michael Francis, Wilderness Society, telephone interview, 6/96.

Timber losses. Randall O'Toole, *Reinventing the Forest Service*, Thoreau Institute, 1995.

Economist quote. Cuff, citing Randall O'Toole.

109. *87% lost money.* Janice Shields, "Timber Sales Losses on Federal lands," press release, 7/7/96.

Tongass background. Cuff.

Paying them to cut trees. O'Toole.

Stevens and Murkowski. Cuff.

Lease extension. Dave Katz, Southeast Alaska Conservation Council, telephone interview, 6/96.

110. *1st ¶.* Chadd.

Special tax breaks. Erlandson.

Ozone tax exemptions

111. *Ozone background. Science News*, 3/20/93.

111–12. *Montreal Protocol, etc.* Erlandson.

112. *Methyl bromide for NAFTA votes.* Alexander Cockburn and Jeffrey St. Clair, "Slime Green," *The Progressive*, 5/96, pp. 18–21.

112–13. *HCFCs. Ozone Action News*, 2/20/95.

A bouquet of miscellaneous rip-offs

Commercial ship subsidies

113. Common Cause, "Common Cause Urges Senate to Act to End Corporate Welfare Programs," press release, 1995.

Fuel efficiency subsidies

The subsidies. Moore and Stansel, *Ending Corporate Welfare as We Know It.*

Big Three propaganda. John Bendel, "Big 3 Plan Escape from CAFE," *North Jersey Herald and News*, 2/18/96.

Advanced tech subsidies

Moore and Stansel, *How Corporate Welfare Won.*

Taxol

114. Janice Shields, "Ending (Corporate) Welfare as We Know It," *Business and Society Review*, Summer 1995.

TAKE THE RICH OFF WELFARE

What we've left out

State and local corporate welfare

115–16. Greg LeRoy, "Terrible Ten 'Candy Store' Deals of 1994; Corporate Welfare At Its Worst," Grassroots Policy Project, press release, 1/23/95.

Easy treatment of white-collar criminals

117. _Crime in the streets vs. suites._ Russell Mokhiber, "Underworld USA," _In These Times_, 4/1–13/96, pp. 14–16.

Medical theft and fraud. L.J. Davis, "Medscam," _Mother Jones_, 3–4/95, pp. 26–29.

Medical negligence. Thomas Maier, "No mortality rate stats for hospitals," _Newsday_, 7/17/95; ABC News, _Nightline_, 7/4/95; _Journal of the AMA_, 7/5/95.

Dangerous or defective products. Russell Mokhiber, _Corporate Crime and Violence_, Sierra Club Books, 1989, p. 16.

118. _Air-bag technology and asbestos._ Mokhiber, "Underworld USA."

Justice Department prosecutions. Mokhiber; Daniel Burnham, "White-Collar Crime: Whitewash at the Justice Department," _Covert Action Quarterly_, Summer 1996.

Horse write-offs

118–19. Barlett, pp. 216–19.

Cut-rate electricity

119–20. Cuff.

Miscellaneous corporate tax breaks

121. _In the 1950s._ Barlett, p. 140.

In the 1990s. Statistical Abstract of the US.

Average earnings. US Bureau of Labor Statistics, Bulletin 2445.

121–22. _Custom legislation._ Barlett, pp. 53–55.

Unlimited interest deductions

122–23. Donald Barlett and James Steele, _America: What Went Wrong?_, Andrews McMeel, 1992, pp. 18–19.

Master limited partnerships

123–24. Barlett and Steele, _America: Who Really Pays the Taxes?_, pp. 156–59.

Low-cost labor

124–25. Randy Albelda, Nancy Folbre and the Center for Popular Economics, *The War on the Poor: A Defense Manual,* The New Press, 1996, p. 67.

Prison labor

125. Christian Parenti, "Making Prison Pay," *The Nation,* 1/29/96, pp. 11–14.

Unicor. Chris Cozzone, "Busted: Corruption at UNICOR," *Prison Life,* 1/95.

Automobile subsidies

125–26. *Cars kill 50,000.* Media Foundation, "The End of the Automotive Age,"
http://www.adbusters.org/~adbusters/main.html

126. *Other costs.* "Mo'slain Greedy sponsored by Slayer's Unltd.," Guerrilla Media, press release, 9/2/95.

126–27. *$1.4-trillion estimate.* Media Foundation.

127–28. *The bus conspiracy.* Mokhiber, *Corporate Crime and Violence,* pp. 221–28.

Welfare for the poor

157–62. Albelda, pp. 132–34; *FY97 Budget; Statistical Abstract of the US.*

INDEX

⟶   ⟶ IF YOU LIKED THIS BOOK,

WHAT UNCLE SAM REALLY WANTS
NOAM CHOMSKY

A brilliant look at the real motivations behind US foreign policy, from the man the *New York Times* called "arguably the most important intellectual alive." 111 pp. $7.   *Highly recommended. —Booklist*

140,000 copies in print

❦

THE PROSPEROUS FEW
AND THE RESTLESS MANY   **NOAM CHOMSKY**

This wide-ranging state-of-the-world report covers everything from Bosnia to biotechnology. Chomsky's fastest-selling book ever. 95 pp. $7.

Calmly reasoned. Most welcome. –Newsday

108,000 copies in print

❦

SECRETS, LIES AND DEMOCRACY
NOAM CHOMSKY

The third in Chomsky's series of state-of-the-world reports, this fascinating book concludes with a list of organizations worth putting time and effort into. 127 pp. $9.

80,000 copies in print

❦

THE CHOMSKY TRILOGY

A boxed set of the three titles above. $20.

❦

THE DECLINE AND FALL
OF THE AMERICAN EMPIRE   **GORE VIDAL**

This delightful book is the perfect introduction to Vidal's witty political writing. 95 pp. $8.

Deliciously, maliciously funny. –NYT Book Review

31,000 copies in print